WHITETAIL TACTICS

❧ WITH ❧

RECURVES & LONGBOWS

◆BOIS◆
d'ARC
PRESS

ACKNOWLEDGEMENTS

Pac Hamblen and the Keith brothers, John and Bob, kindly shared not only their perceptive observations of deer but also their beautiful ranches.

Special thanks to peerless photographer Mike Biggs for providing the deer photos.

Bowhunting wouldn't be half the fun without compadres Paul and Ted Crow, Jim Welch, Brad Smith, Frank Sherwood, Paul Brunner, Steve Dollar, and Barry Hardin.

TABLE OF CONTENTS

For Dad, who introduced me to

Professor Whitetail at a tender age.

WHITETAIL TACTICS
with
RECURVES & LONGBOWS

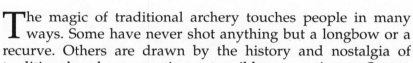

The magic of traditional archery touches people in many ways. Some have never shot anything but a longbow or a recurve. Others are drawn by the history and nostalgia of traditional archery, wanting a tangible connection to Saxton Pope, Arthur Young, Fred Bear, and the Native American hunters who are the true pioneers of today's bowhunting.

No matter how you start with a recurve or longbow, what keeps us hooked is the fun and challenge of hunting with one of these venerable weapons. A traditional bow is to hunting what a flyrod is to fishing, as much an attitude as anything else. A simple stick and string allows men to become an integral part of the natural world. With a modern, scope-equipped rifle, a hunter is lethal out to three or four hundred yards; with a muzzleloader out to at least a hundred; with a compound bow kills at fifty yards are commonplace. But with the self-imposed limitations of a longbow or recurve, the hunter must slip undetected inside a deer's defenses, within fifteen yards, "wolf range," where deer are bred to watch for danger.

To growing numbers of archers, becoming such a consummate predator is the ultimate challenge. Just seeing deer at a distance is no longer good enough, to get within longbow range you must know exactly where deer will be and when they will be there. You have to pinpoint their movements to within a few yards. You have to have A Plan.

That's what this book is all about.

Years ago I came to the realization that hunting whitetails with a longbow was a disease, and that the sooner I learned all I could about it the better my chances of staying solvent,

staying married, and staying sane. Like many others, I've absorbed anything I could find from books, magazines, and other whitetail hunters equally infected. But most of all I've learned from the deer. Anyone who successfully hunts whitetails, and especially large, mature bucks, eventually develops his own unique methods for getting hunter and hunted together.

The tools and tactics contained herein have all been repeatedly proven in the field. These methods will get you close to deer. Which is not to say that they are some kind of magic bullet, for the "experts," including this one, still get skunked more often than not. The quarry is incredibly wary and adaptable and has senses far beyond our own. Using a traditional bow in a quest for deer will prove beyond a doubt that the sport is all about *hunting* and not *killing*.

But when you finally kneel down next to that hard-earned buck, the one you scouted and out-foxed and practiced so long for, you'll be ruined for life.

Just ask the wife of any successful traditional bowhunter.

EQUIPMENT

Though the equipment is relatively simple—which is, in fact, part of the appeal of longbows and recurves—this section is fairly extensive. There are many options and details from which to choose, and when trying to place oneself within arrow range of a buck who acts as though he was born with a nervous breakdown, the tiny details make all the difference.

Brand names of equipment will be mentioned here and throughout the remainder of the book. I may as well state now that I'm not receiving a farthing from the manufacturers for these endorsements. Not one cent. I mention the various products simply because over the years I have found them to be especially well-suited to the exacting art of bowhunting. The company names and addresses are listed together in the appendix.

MAPS

That's right—maps.

They may be the single most important piece of equipment in a bowhunter's bag of tricks. If you want to consistently kill deer a topographic map along with an aerial photo are as invaluable as a sharp broadhead. Don't scrimp on maps. Both a topo map and aerial photo are essential for pinning down deers' locations; the first shows elevations and the second vegetation. More about how to implement them as part of The Plan in a later section.

Aerial photos are available from commercial firms in larger cities. Look in the Yellow Pages under Photographers—Aerial. You can check their master photos and pinpoint the exact area you want. A scale of 1" to 600' gives plenty of detail; you can usually discern individual trees. The photo should extend approximately a mile beyond your boundaries, for it is important to understand what is happening around your hunting property as well as within it.

Most Soil Conservation Service offices have color aerial photos of their area updated a couple of times a year. They may or may not allow you to use their negative to make your own photo, but they are definitely worth a try. If all else fails, you and your hunting partners can charter a small plane and make your own high-altitude pictures. Be sure to fly high enough so that the property around your hunting ground is included in the photo. Divided among several people the cost will be well within reason for a place hunted year after year.

An aerial photo is as indispensible as a sharp broadhead.

Color topographic maps are printed and distributed by the U.S. Geological Survey. They can be ordered directly from the government if you know exactly the quadrangle you need. Also order a map legend, which details the symbols used on the maps. Check the white pages (larger cities will have a blue section in the phone book for government numbers) under United States Government Offices, Interior Department, Geological Survey. Or contact the U.S. Geological Survey, Box 25286, Federal Center Building #41, Denver, CO, 80225.

If you're allergic to the government's red-tape and propensity for screw-ups, the simplest way to obtain maps in metropolitan areas is from a commercial distributor, in the yellow pages under Maps—Dealer. You can check his master map and select precisely the area you need. Buy the large scale topos of 7.5 minutes.

If you're not currently using these tools, get a map and a photo for every area you hunt. A custom black and white photo will run from $25 to $75, depending upon where you obtain it, and a topographic map about $5 per quadrangle. This will be the most effective money you've ever spent on hunting equipment. Trust me on this one.

BOWS

Many a verbal fistfight has begun over a discussion of bow design and shooting characteristics. Experienced traditional archers probably already have opinions set in concrete, and that's understandable, for we tend to believe in what works for us. Which brings up an important point. The number one goal in traditional bowhunting is precisely placing an arrow into the kill area of a game animal. If this can be accomplished with a forty-year-old $5 garage sale recurve or a freshly cut willow branch, great. Use whatever works for you and hold your head high.

That said, this section should help the beginner narrow down his options and perhaps expose the old-timer to a new trick or two.

All things considered, a recurve is probably the easiest to learn, and may be the best choice for the compound shooter sampling traditional bows for the first time. Recurves are shorter, and because the limb tips turn away from the shooter, they possess greater speed per pound of draw weight than a straight-limbed bow, about 175 feet per second for a fifty-five pound bow. This yields a flatter trajectory than a longbow and makes aiming easier at longer distances. But the entire point of the exercise lies in getting close, under twenty yards, so a flat trajectory becomes almost irrelevant.

Most recurves are center-shot, like a compound, and the arrow does not have to bend or negotiate the paradox around the handle. This makes the bow "point" more naturally for the beginner. Most recurves also have a pistol-grip style handle, again like a compound, and shoot very smoothly with little hand-shock.

Some recurves come in "take-down" models, whose limbs detach for easier transportation. This could be a consideration for those using horses, backpacking, or canoeing into a hunting area. And for airline travel a take-down is a natural, since even a creative baggage handler will have a difficult time destroying one.

Take-downs can also be purchased with limbs of different weights, a clear advantage. Use limbs of moderate pull weight in the beginning, until you grow comfortable with the bow and your shooting form is second nature. Then, substitute limbs five or ten pounds heavier. Different weights can also be used for different applications: fifty pounds for a day of roving or deer hunting, sixty-five pounds for heavy-boned game such as bear or moose.

Though recurves have some advantages, many traditional shooters lean toward longbows. Though not quite as fast as a recurve, a fifty-pound longbow shoots a hunting weight arrow about 150 feet per second, making a permanent believer out of any whitetail crossing its path. The longer limbs stabilize the bow, thus making it more forgiving of slight errors in grip or release. And with the knee-buckling adrenaline deluge which often *tilts* a bowhunter's shooting form during a "whites of the eyes" encounter, we need all the forgiveness in our weapons we can get. This adds up to more consistent accuracy for most shooters, especially at hunting ranges, one of the primary reasons the longbow design has survived for the past three hundred generations.

Don't let the "long" in longbow concern you. Light and graceful in the hand, they lend themselves to quick, instinctive shots, the rule rather than the exception in the field. In a fiber-glass laminated bow, I prefer the longer designs, 66 or 68" in length, which yield a silky-smooth draw and consistent accuracy. No matter what the shooting position: tree stand, kneeling, or sitting, their length is rarely unwieldy.

We could easily get side-tracked here into a discussion of fiberglass laminations, glue-line thicknesses, and even self bows made from a single piece of wood split from a tree trunk. But since this book is about bowhunting and not bowmaking, we'll instead focus our attention on bow characteristics which can affect the outcome of a hunt.

Whichever style of bow you finally choose, its weight should be easy and comfortable to shoot. That's right, *easy* to shoot. Don't get caught up in the testosterone-induced fantasy that a bow must pull seventy pounds to be effective. Accuracy is far and away the most important aspect of archery, and it is impossible to shoot accurately if a bow is too heavy. If you are just beginning with a longbow or recurve, please, please (I'm writing this from my knees), don't start with more than fifty pounds. A fifty pound bow will allow you to kill any deer in this country, *if* the arrow is placed in the old boiler-works. And for the vast majority of hunters, myself included, that's far more likely with a fifty pound bow which is comfortable to shoot than with an unmanageable seventy pound beast.

Naturally, a heavier bow shoots an arrow faster, but the extra speed is purchased at a high cost. A fifty pound longbow shoots a six hundred grain arrow about 150 fps, a seventy pound bow about 178 fps. The stronger bow is about 19% faster but becomes 40% harder to pull, not a very good trade-off if your accuracy suffers. If you demand more speed but at a comfortable draw weight, then consider a recurve.

A friend who is a reformed compound shooter recently harvested his first animal with a fifty-three pound longbow, a big cow elk. He never saw the arrow strike her, and thought at first he'd missed completely. Within five seconds she went down. He thought she was simply bedding down, and was astonished when he realized she was quite deceased. I examined the skinned carcass the next day. The arrow had split one rib on entry and glanced off of another on exit, having passed entirely through the elk. You'll not find a stronger advocate of mid-weight longbows than my friend.

You should be able to shoot your traditional bow at least fifty times without growing fatigued. If not, then the bow is too heavy, no matter what its weight, and when you inevitably find it inconsistent you'll be tempted to pitch it, sell it, or give it to your brother-in-law. I've known many dedicated traditional archers who would be marvelous shots if only they used a fifty pound bow instead of one seventy pounds. It is far better to shoot a bow ten pounds too light than five pounds too heavy, for the five extra pounds will seem like twenty-five after you've been sitting in a treestand for three hours in the sleet and would very much like to shoot that trophy buck trotting past.

Where to buy a bow? Three major mail-order companies carry weapons from numerous bowyers, allowing you to easily compare color photos of different bows, their options, and prices. Three Rivers Archery, Kustom King, and Butler's offer catalogs.

In addition to custom bows, Three Rivers Archery also offers production bows from Bear Archery. Fred Bear patented the use of fiberglass in bows in the early 1950's, and he spent a lifetime perfecting a one-piece recurve which starts for around two hundred and fifty dollars, a lot of bow for the money and an excellent choice.

BOW SETUP

Experienced hunters, no matter what type of weapon they shoot, eventually learn that a quiet bow may be second only to accuracy on a list of bow attributes, certainly ranking well ahead of speed when it comes to taking big game.

Consider this: The speed of sound is about 1100 feet per second. A fifty pound longbow shoots about 150 fps, a fifty pound recurve about 175 fps, and a top of the line fifty pound compound about 300 fps, all just a fraction of the speed of sound. If a deer hears the release of an arrow, he WILL reflexively jump, no matter what kind of bow is used. You can't beat a deer's reflexes with speed, but you can with silence. If he doesn't hear the shot he can't react.

The most common noise reducers are string silencers. Silencers are available in several styles: strands of carpet, rubber "spiders," or long strips of fur such as otter wrapped around or through the string about eight inches from each tip.

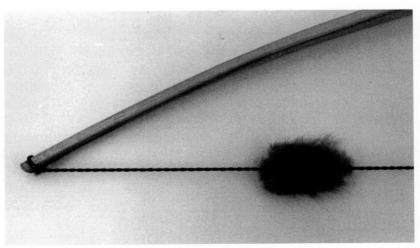

A strip of otter fur wrapped around the string to dampen noise.

Though natural fur is the most attractive on a traditional bow, all work by breaking up and dampening the waves of energy left behind after the release of an arrow. Most of the energy a bow stores during the draw transfers to the arrow, but some remains behind as handshock and, worst of all, game-alerting noise. Instead of a sharp vibrating "twang," with silencers the string whispers only a soft "bemp."

Making a bow more efficient—which means less energy left behind to foster noise—can be as simple as shooting a heavier arrow. Such an arrow not only yields greater penetration by draining extra energy from the bow, it also shoots more quietly with less handshock. Try shooting 400 and 600 grain arrows from a fifty pound bow and listen to the difference. You'll like what you don't hear with the heavier arrow.

Incorrect brace height of a traditional bow remains one of the worst single offenders at creating noise, as it forces the arrow to slap the side of the sight window as it bends around the handle. This is caused by stringing the bow too low, or with the string too close to the handle. A low strung bow has some advantages, such as slightly higher arrow speed, so the brace height should be raised a small amount at a time—by unstringing the bow and twisting the string a couple of times—until the noise is eliminated. Arrow flight should improve, too. In general, a bow should be strung as low as possible while still giving clean arrow flight with no slap on release. Brace height is different for every bow, arrow design, and release technique and requires individual adjustment.

This slapping problem can also be caused by incorrectly spined arrows, or arrows either too stiff or too limber. Longbows, whether made from one piece of wood or from fiberglass laminations, are usually not centershot, meaning the arrow must bend around the handle upon release. Arrows which are too stiff, or spined too heavy, are worse about creating noise because they cannot flex around the handle. It should be noted that recurves are generally centershot and thus more tolerant of a wider range of arrow spines.

The shelf and the arrow plate, which lie on the inside of the sight window, require padding to reduce noise. Some type of rug or fur is often used on the shelf, but leather, or one of the commercial "stick-on" felt or fur tabs, can be glued to the arrow plate to eliminate the sound of the shaft and feathers sliding past the bow.

On a related subject, a nocked arrow's feathers should not touch the bow or the bow hand. The practically inaudible (to us) sound of vanes dragging across the shelf as the arrow is drawn becomes an almost certain kiss of death. And I don't mean to the deer. A couple of bow seasons ago, one of the biggest whitetail bucks I've ever seen in the wild sauntered past at seven yards. For once, things had gone perfectly, and I had him ambushed at dusk between his bedding area in heavy cedars and the wheat field where he was feeding at night. The massive ten-pointer never had a hint that I was almost literally breathing down his neck. I had done everything right—except for one microscopic oversight. My bow was strung slightly low, enough so that the feathers of my arrow barely touched the arrow shelf and made the faintest of rustles as I began the draw. He wasn't sure what made the sound, but he knew for sure he didn't like it and gave a couple of tremendous bounds to one side before stopping thirty-five yards away in the brush. He stood as if frozen for five minutes, and the image is forever burned into my mind. Never suspecting that he had just avoid-ed feathered death by the slimmest of margins, he finally continued calmly on his way. That was the only time this specific problem has cost me a shot at game, but you may wager your last nickel that the feathers of my hunting arrows no longer touch my bow.

A shiny new bow may look great to us, but deer, and big bucks especially, don't like them nearly as well. In fact, they like a shiny bow so little that they generally leave like a scalded bat if they see one in the woods. Very fine steel wool will dull the shine on a bow without jeopardizing the finish. Some glue snakeskins to the back of their bow, giving it a very business-like appearance. Camo tape is a simpler solution; just apply it to the back of the bow and trim the edges.

One last detail to add to your bow is a wind feather. I know they look a little goofy, but since we spend most of our time trying to overcome a deer's first line of defense, his nose, keeping track of wind currents and eddies is crucial. A wind feather permits constant monitoring of the wind while you move through the woods or sit in a treestand, a much better option than licking your finger or fogging talcum powder from a small plastic bottle. Simply tie one end of a six inch length of thread or dental floss to a fluff feather (available from archery catalogs or craft supply shops), and loop the other end a couple of times through your unstrung bowstring near the upper tip. For some reason, veteran hunters in particular are resistant to trying a wind feather for the first time, but once they use one for a single afternoon's hunt they'll never be without one again.

A wind feather on a thread attached to the bowstring.

ARROWS

While aluminum arrows will, technically, shoot from a long-bow or recurve, they often sound like dropping a 9/16" wrench onto a concrete floor. In comparison, wooden arrows are deathly quiet. Besides, they fly perfectly, look great, and just seem to go with a traditional bow.

For those only beginning with longbows or recurves, the arrow length will normally be shorter by a couple of inches as compared to shooting a compound. With an instinctive shooting style, you "lean" into the draw, thus slightly shortening arrow length. Though I have ridiculously long arms, wearing a 37" sleeve, I've learned to comfortably and consistently shoot a 28 1/2" arrow.

Consistent accuracy is impossible if the arrows are not matched and do not fly straight—try shooting a group from your favorite rifle with half a dozen different brands of ammunition and you'll see what I mean. Beyond accuracy, hunters have an additional reason for insisting on true arrow flight, since an arrow which wobbles in the air sheds more speed, or energy, resulting in decreased penetration.

Arrow flight begins with the spine, or stiffness, of the arrow shaft, because the arrow must flex, then recover when released. Based on a standard 28" draw length, wooden arrows are sorted into five pound increments corresponding to the weight of the bow. For example, a fifty-eight pound center shot longbow requires arrows spined for fifty-five to sixty pounds. Keep in mind that spine figures should be adjusted based on your draw length: For each inch of length over 28", add five pounds of spine; for each inch under 28", subtract five. With the above example, a bow which draws fifty-eight pounds at 27" requires five pounds less spine or fifty to fifty-five pound arrows. Arrows for an extra-fast recurve or with heavy broadheads, because of the extra stress on the wood, need an additional five pounds of spine. For non-center shot bows such as all-wood self bows, I've found that arrows spined five pounds *lighter* than the figures given above fly better because they have a bit more flex to bend around the handle.

Penetration on game is essential, and arrow weight should

be considered as a major factor. Shoot a 600 grain and a 400 grain arrow from the same bow. The lighter arrow flies noticeably faster, but the heavier arrow, though a bit slower, yields considerably greater penetration. As an example, kinetic energy is calculated by multiplying arrow speed by arrow speed by arrow weight. Then divide by 450,000 to yield foot pounds of energy. Shot from a fifty pound longbow, a 600 grain arrow flies about 150 feet per second and a 400 grain arrow about 160 fps. These numbers yield a kinetic energy figure of 22.7 foot pounds of energy for the light arrow and 30.0 for the heavy one, a whopping 32% advantage. This occurs because a heavier arrow drains more energy from the bow, making it more efficient, the same reason a heavier arrow reduces hand shock and quietens a bow. The penetration value of heavier arrows is often overlooked in the modern quest for ever greater arrow speeds. This is especially important when shooting down on an animal from a treestand or other elevation, when an exit wound can very well make the difference between an easy to follow blood trail and no trail at all.

So, if the hunter brings his predatory juices to a boil and works in closely, twenty yards or less, heavier arrows give away nothing in accuracy and offer far more penetration—the name of the game. A useful rule of thumb when ordering arrows is at least ten grains of arrow weight (including the point) for each pound of bow weight.

A commercial arrow-maker such as Kustom King can help you choose arrows over the phone, or better yet, a good archery shop should have wooden arrows of different spines and weights available to actually shoot and match to the bow.

As for nocks, you have two basic choices: a clip-on nock, which gently clamps onto the string, and a speed nock which fits the string loosely. Though largely a matter of individual preference, clip-on nocks may be more desirable for the hunter because they keep the arrow in place on the string during long periods of waiting on a stand (for this reason, most traditional hunters prefer to nock an arrow under the nocking marker on the string instead of above, since the weight of the shaft and point levering over the arrow rest pushes the nock against the nocking marker and holds the arrow in place). The nock color is usually chosen for compatibility with the crown dip and cresting colors, but keep in mind that white, yellow, or even fluorescent green will show up more readily in flight as well as in the target.

For a three feather fletch, center-shot recurves generally shoot a five inch parabolic, or banana cut, flawlessly. But for a non center-shot bow such as a laminated longbow or wooden self-bow, more feather is required to stabilize the arrow as it recovers from bending around the handle. A five and a half inch shield-cut feather is a long-time favorite. Your arrowmaker can offer guidance in this regard, though remember that more feather instead of less is the most forgiving in crosswinds or wet weather. Ask him (or her) to put the feathers on with some helical so the arrow will spin in flight and stabilize like a rifle bullet.

Real barred turkey feathers, because of their traditional look and great popularity, have become relatively scarce and expensive. Dyed domestic turkey feathers are readily available, and the colors can be chosen to match the cresting on the arrow. Feather color can be especially critical to a hunter. In low light conditions, seeing the location of a hit on an animal can tell you when to back off and wait before following the trail, as with a liver shot, for example. Yellow and white fletching shows up fairly well under these conditions, but light blue, with a yellow or white cock feather, works best of all and looks like a tracer on its way to the target.

Once the arrows are properly matched to the bow, some final bow set-up solves any additional difficulties. Arrows which porpoise in flight, or wobble up and down, are caused by an improper nocking point. Using a bow-square, the nocking point should be placed on the string about 3/8" above the arrow shelf of the bow, then the arrow nocked underneath this point. If porpoising persists, move the nock up slightly until the problem disappears.

A fishtail, or side to side wobble in flight, is usually caused by improper arrow spine or insufficient fletching, but it can also be caused by a too-low brace height. Six to six and a quarter inches between the string and bow is about right. Raise the brace height an eighth of an inch at a time until the arrows fly straight and true.

BROADHEADS

Traditional hunters, almost to a man, have come to rely upon a single-blade broadhead of sturdy design. Every broadhead on the market today has its adherents and promoters, but contemporary wisdom and expensive four-color magazine ads alone make little impression on trophy bucks. What will impress them is a broadhead which gives consistent performance in the field, and by choosing one you tip the scales of success in your favor.

With all of the hype which currently surrounds bowhunting, it is easy to lose sight of the true objective, which has remained the same all the way down from the first squint-eyed cavemen to the present day: penetrating a vital area of an animal with a razor-sharp cutting surface.

How best to accomplish this?

At first glance, it seems that if a single blade broadhead is good, then three, four, or even six are better, providing a greatly increased cutting area and more potential for inflicting mortal damage. In 1985, Ed Ashby conducted extensive tests at the Mkuzi Game Preserve in South Africa to determine the effectiveness of thirty-two different broadheads. He thoroughly tested single and multi-bladed heads against African game weighing one hundred to one thousand pounds. His study produced some eye-openers. "...When a bone of any type is hit, the single blade head offers vastly superior penetration. Even with a soft tissue hit, the single blade heads penetrate substantially better..." Ashby finally concluded that, "...there is a significant reduction in the percentage of shots reaching a lethal area with multiblade heads."

A reduction in the percentage of lethal hits can only mean a reduction in game taken by the hunter using multi-bladed heads. The additional sharp edges of this style of point perform little service if they cannot reliably penetrate. If you simply must have additional cutting surface, the small replaceable "bleeder" type of inserts set into a broadhead are perhaps the least detrimental to performance. But even these restrict penetration to some degree.

Which leaves us with the time-tested, V-shaped, basic steel broadhead as the most consistently effective, the same one which has been used for a thousand years and a close relative to ancient stone points. There are a few subtle variations available which should be considered.

Single blade broadheads are available with concave, convex, or straight edges; choosing one becomes largely a matter of personal preference. A concave shape, with the sides slightly sweeping in toward the ferrule, such as the one Howard Hill designed, is the most difficult to sharpen. Relatively easier is a convex point with the sides slightly flaring out like the Bear Razorhead, which has probably taken as much game as any other single broadhead. But the simplest and easiest of all to sharpen remains the broadhead with straight sides such as a Zwickey or Magnus.

The ideal length to width ratio of the point has long been argued. Howard Hill maintained the ratio should be 3-1 so the broadhead would not windplane, or dart and dive in flight. A head of this length requires reinforcement near the point, so it will not fold over if it strikes a bone. An excellent point of this design is the Grizzly—straight cutting edges, a reinforced tip, and length three times the width—which was one of the best performers in the tests conducted by Ashby. I've always had good luck with this broadhead, too, though the tip is quite blunt for my tastes and sharpening it to a needle point takes considerable filing.

A 2.5-1 length to width ratio flies flawlessly as well, and is a bit less prone to damage upon striking bone. A Wolverine, Magnus, or one of the excellent Zwickey broadheads (all without the optional bleeder blades, please) fall into this category.

Two time-tested broadheads; the Magnus, left, and Zwickey, right.

I've used Zwickey Eskimo points for years, and know without question they consistently put meat on the pole.

It's impossible to overemphasis the importance of super-sharp broadheads for hunting. A well-honed point slices everything it touches, killing quickly and cleanly, while a dull edge just pushes vitals aside as it passes, leading to wounded game and non-existent blood trails, the nightmare of every bowhunter. There can be no excuse for doing everything right—months of practice, slipping to within bow range, and making a perfect pressure shot— only to lose a beautiful game animal due to improperly sharpened broadheads. If you're not afraid of the edge, then it's not sharp enough.

The easiest and perhaps oldest way to sharpen a single-blade broadhead is with a small bastard file. Smoothly stroke the file into the edge of the broadhead at a fairly flat angle, from base to tip. Four surfaces, two on each edge, must be beveled. Different broadheads are often of different steel and different hardness, so it sometimes takes a bit of experimentation to find the correct angle and pressure to produce an edge. A new file purchased before each hunting season makes the sharpening much easier.

A Tru-angle hone, flat file, and diamond steel. The Tru-angle gives the fastest, most consistently razor-sharp edge of any method the author has found.

The file-sharpened edge will have tiny, razor-sharp serrations, which many old-timers felt stayed sharp even after contact with hair or bone. If you want a smoother edge, a round diamond steel works well. You will also find it useful if you encounter difficulty obtaining a sharp broadhead with file alone—a few strokes with the steel smoothes out any tiny burrs along the edge.

If holding the file at the proper angle gives you problems, try a Tru-angle hone: two files screwed to a piece of wood which has been beveled. Once the angle has been established on a new broadhead, there is a trick to sharpening. Flip the point over after every pass down the files, and use progressively lighter and lighter pressure until, on the final pass after thirty strokes or so, just the weight of the broadhead and arrow are felt against the files. Strop the point on a leather boot top a few times and you have a wickedly sharp cutting surface. This is by far my favorite method for it is quick and produces the most consistent edge.

A power wet-grinder can produce a fairly sharp edge, though it will need some final touch-up with a file or diamond steel. This tool is most useful for placing an initial edge on new broadheads. Another power device is a knife-sharpening felt wheel on a grinder. If you follow the manufacturer's instructions, this buffer gives an extraordinarily smooth, sharp edge. Of course, you should never use a regular grinder on a broadhead as the heat generated destroys the temper.

The standard flat diamond steels or Arkansas stones can also be used for broadheads, though you'll find this method much slower than the file or power tools. A helpful accessory is an angle guide, a device clamped to the broadhead to ensure a consistent honing angle against the stone.

A broadhead must easily shave hair before it's taken to the woods and should be resharpened as needed to keep it that way. Remember, if you're not afraid of the edge, it's not sharp enough.

QUIVERS

Since the advent of the bow some ten or fifteen thousand years ago, archers have faced the vexing problem of carrying arrows. From the earliest prehistoric hunter wandering across the snow-blasted European landscape, to an Englishman gripping his longbow at the battle of Agincourt, to an American Indian easing through a glade in the forest, various quivers were tried. They were all inventive but never came up with the perfect solution to the arrow problem.

And so it is today.

An ideal quiver should possess several different and at times conflicting traits. Arrows must be readily available, yet protected. They must be held securely and quietly, yet be easily extracted. The quiver has to be comfortable and hold an adequate number of arrows, but keep the deadly points safely away from the archer. Considering these schizophrenic requirements, it seems natural that today's bowhunters should still struggle with quiver design.

We have available several quivers based upon those passed down from ancient times along with a couple of modern innovations.

Probably most familiar to a traditionalist is the back quiver, seasoned with the lore of yew longbows, Sherwood Forest, and archery's bygone days. It should be no surprise that this type of quiver has been used for centuries, since it has so many positive attributes.

A back quiver holds plenty of arrows at the ready just over the right shoulder, up to fifteen or twenty for a day of roving where many different points may be needed. It also carries arrows comfortably and unobtrusively—you hardly know it's there. Even in a treestand a back quiver is a natural, since the strap hangs over the seat, leaving the arrows within easy reach of the right hand.

A back quiver looks great and is convenient, but makes noise in thick brush and doesn't protect fletching from rain.

But perhaps best of all, a well-oiled leather back quiver just *goes* with a traditional bow. Looks and feel are high on the list for those practical romantics who choose a longbow or recurve, and this quiver fits the bill.

Along with all of the positives, there is, I'm afraid, at least one important negative. A back quiver holds the feathered ends of the arrows just above the right shoulder, where they constantly snag on brush or low-hanging limbs. This not only tends to damage the feathers but creates noise: quietly stalking through thick timber while wearing one of these quivers becomes next to impossible. Though fine for all-around use, other designs stand superior for hunting purposes.

One of these is the Indian-style quiver. Supported by a strap over the left shoulder, this holds the arrows horizontally across the back where they ride quietly and comfortably. When hunting or stalking, the strap is switched to the right shoulder, and the quiver carried at the waist on the left side leaving arrows at the immediate ready. This design, because of its utility, is one of the oldest. In fact, it may be *the* oldest. The so-called Iceman, the prehistoric man recently found entombed in a glacier in Italy, carried a deerskin quiver of this design. At 5,300 years old, it represents the most ancient quiver ever found.

The only drawback I can find to this design is that it's not commercially available at present, though this should be no obstacle to most traditional hunters who are intent on making most if not all of their own tackle anyway. A few hours spent with leather, needle, and thread yields a versatile quiver whose lineage stretches back to the dawn of archery.

Another design used for a few thousand years is the belt quiver which hangs at the right hip. English yeomen with their longbows, mounted Japanese warriors, and many Native American hunters all preferred the belt quiver. Today, a belt quiver is excellent for target shooting or roving, as the arrows are instantly available and quick to replace after retrieval. Though I use one almost exclusively for practice shooting, I've also found it works reasonably well for hunting. This design ranks well ahead of a back quiver when it comes to moving silently through brush, as the right hand can rest on the arrows to guide them and prevent rattling.

In modern times, some new designs have been introduced to the age-old problem of carrying arrows.

The bow quiver has become a popular alternative due to its convenience—if you have a bow you automatically have arrows. This design attaches to a bow with straps, Velcro, or by fitting over the limbs of a longbow or recurve (some recurves offer an optional bow quiver, which bolts to the bow). Such quivers generally come in two parts, one hooded to protect the user from broadheads, and the other with slots to securely hold the arrow shafts. A bow quiver keeps arrows handy, perhaps more so than any other design. But they are also more exposed to damage and—worst of all—making noise, the bane of every bowhunter. This type of quiver makes a bow heavier, and to some shooters unbalances a bow, though this is a matter of individual tastes. While one of the most convenient and practical, a bow quiver is also my least favorite, but primarily from an aesthetic standpoint. It diminishes the looks of a bow by spoiling the graceful lines, and while recognizing that looks kill few game animals, I'm still mildly offended by it. But for the more pragmatic, a bow quiver remains a viable choice.

I normally drag my feet when confronted with radical innovations in archery convention, but have made an exception in the case of center-back quivers, a real step forward in quiver design. Glenn St. Charles, one of the founders of the Pope and Young Club, invented this quiver in the 1950's and Fred Bear offered it in his catalog as the "St. Charles quiver." This design holds arrows down the center of the hunter's back with the feathers up. The feathers lie completely enclosed and protected by a hood, eliminating two previous problems with carrying arrows: noise when moving through the woods and wet fletching during rain. A hunting companion once returned to a rainy camp with a yellow bread sack tied over the arrows in his backquiver, an expedient we (and probably the deer) found hilarious. A St. Charles quiver neatly solves this problem.

Arrows are placed into this quiver feathers first as the nocks are pressed upward into foam rubber, then the points are seated into hard rubber at the bottom. The pressure from the foam holds the arrows securely. The archer simply reaches behind

The best all-around hunting quiver ever devised, the Catquiver by Rancho Safari.

and grasps a shaft, lifts up on it slightly so the tip clears its base, then quietly withdraws it to the side.

With the flood of technology which began inundating archery thirty years ago, the need for traditional tackle flickered and faded, and the St. Charles quiver was no longer produced. In the last few years, however, with the overwhelming rediscovery of the personal satisfaction of longbows and recurves, I'm delighted to report that these quivers with a leather hood are once again available, made by Glenn St. Charles and his sons. Another version of this design, made by Rancho Safari and known as the Catquiver, offers pockets and pouches in various configurations and allows the quiver to double as a daypack or light overnight pack. The Catquiver's pockets are great for holding hunting license, camera, and an extra bowstring. Both of these modern offerings are well designed and perfectly matched to a longbow or recurve—and this from one who prides himself on his Old Maid attitudes about traditional archery.

The only drawback to this St. Charles style quiver is that arrows are difficult to replace without removing it from your back. For roving or practice where arrows are constantly being fired and returned to the quiver this can be a serious inconvenience, though such a limitation won't trouble hunters.

Purely for hunting, a St. Charles style quiver has no equal, carrying broadhead arrows quietly, safely, and dryly. This type of quiver is all but a necessity.

TREESTANDS

Treestands are simply a portable platform which allow a hunter to sit in a tree in safety and reasonable comfort. It's only fair to state that some traditional hunters look upon treestands as the epitome of modern technological shortcuts, degrading bowhunting by taking the place of skill and dedication. They sometimes quote the legendary Saxton Pope, who in 1925 wrote, "We scorned to shoot from a tree." With this edict, they consider the case closed.

Perhaps, before continuing, we should look more closely at the historical precedents.

Dr. Pope's reference to hunting from trees involved not deer, but grizzly bears which he and Arthur Young hunted in present-day Yellowstone Park. In a tree, there was no danger from the bear, and hunting from the ground added, as Pope said modestly, "zest" to the chase. Saxton Pope and Arthur Young are two of my heroes, and stand today as the grandfathers of modern bowhunting, but we should also note that they routinely took seventy and eighty yard "Hail Mary" shots at game, wouldn't dream of shooting a doe, and regularly shot quail on the ground, all of which today would be considered very bad form indeed.

I suppose, in the end, that everyone has to examine the evidence in light of today's conservation ethics and make up his own mind about the morality of a particular practice, the use of treestands among them. As for myself, it's difficult to discern the moral difference between using a chain-on stand and balancing like an acrobat on a tree branch in an attempt to get close to deer as have hunters for the past few millennia. Maybe my sentiments on the subject can best be stated this way: For a traditional archer, I'm about as hard-core as they come, hunting by choice with an Osage Orange flatbow (much like Art Young's favorite bow), and have, on occasion, taken deer with flint points mounted on hand-made dogwood arrows. And I not only regularly hunt from a treestand, but delight in it. An improperly placed treestand or one manned by an inattentive hunter is a waste of time, anyway, so they are certainly no sure-fire shortcut to success.

The most common treestand design consists of a seat and a platform for the feet mounted on a vertical frame, all of which securely attaches to the tree with a chain or strap. I prefer the chain-on variety rather than the strap-on variety, for they are quieter and more secure. Some of the strap-ons are so unstable they would give a trapeze artist the queezies. You'll find chain-ons available through larger retail archery shops and advertisers in bowhunting magazines. I've used these stands for years, in both seated and standing positions, and I can shoot a 68" longbow from them easily. The chain-ons require a straight tree, or at least a straight section six to eight feet long, which makes it a natural for the West with its pines and firs, the midwest with its cottonwoods, and also the East with its pine and hardwood forests.

The Trophy Whitetail stand locks firmly to a tree when the platform is pressed into position. Note padded seat with adjustable height.

Wedge-Loc's patented system for hanging the stand from the harness—stable and safe.

I judge a treestand by its stability and comfort, and my two favorite chain-ons are made by Trophy Whitetail and Wedge-Loc. The Trophy Whitetail stand has a unique cam action which secures it to the tree and makes the platform exceptionally stable. The padded, waterproof seat adjusts in height and is the most comfortable I've ever used. Wedge-Loc's Brute stand has both a roomy platform and an ample seat. On trees over 8" in diameter, for which it was designed, this stand is also rock-solid. Anyone who soon grows restless and starts fidgeting in a treestand should try a Trophy Whitetail or a Wedge-Loc. They are the most comfortable, secure stands on the market.

In places like central and western Texas, where you can spend half a day searching for a straight tree, a chain-on has fairly limited use, which is why I use a fork stand extensively. These small platforms have a piano hinge across the middle and spikes on each end. The hunter places the stand, slightly folded, in the fork of a tree. He then pushes the center of the stand downward which drives the spikes securely into the wood as the platform flattens and locks into position. I've

A fork stand has a hinge arrangement and spikes on each end. When the platform is pressed into position, the spikes hold the stand securely in the tree.

found fork stands to be excellent for gnarled trunks such as liveoaks and Spanish oaks, and it is the rare tree which won't accept one. Bear River is one of several manufacturers who offer this type stand.

I've employed both chain-on and fork stands in a great variety of terrains and applications and highly recommend them for the traditional bowhunter. A third style of stand is the self-climber, which manually climbs a tree every time you use it. It has numerous drawbacks. Self-climbers in general are clumsy, noisy, require a straight tree with no side branches to function, and can be hazardous if they slip during mid-climb.

Which brings up a crucial point—safety.

Manufacturer's instructions were written so you won't get hurt and they won't get sued. Their installation procedures should always be carefully followed. And always, always wear a safety harness both when placing a stand and when using it for hunting. There is nothing the least bit funny about falling twenty feet out of tree: a stand can break, a hunter can fall asleep, or slip, or step right off the edge in his excitement over a big buck. Real-life horror stories crop up every year about hunters who have broken legs, arms, and necks when not wearing a safety harness. An additional word of caution about fork stands: Don't place one between two trees, for in a high wind the trees may blow in opposite directions, dropping the stand and possibly one very surprised hunter.

With the chance of slips, even with a safety belt, the deadliness of a razor-sharp broadhead takes on an added lethal dimension. Do not carry the bow and quiver up the tree but pull them up with a line after you safely secure yourself to the stand with a harness. Lower them the same way before you climb down.

For those of us who aren't as slim or as agile as we once were, ladder stands are a great alternative to chain-on or fork stands. They're quick to put up and both safe and easy to enter. Though a bit more obtrusive than a treestand, careful site selection with cover such as cedars or pines to help hide the ladder more than compensates. Big Buck's Phantom folding ladder stand is relatively easy to conceal in the woods because the ladder fits close against the tree. The Phantom includes backpack straps for carrying. I also like Bear River's Big Bear stand for its size and comfort; this is one of the few stands in which you could reasonably spend an entire day.

I'm a great believer in having multiple stands, as many as fifteen or twenty if hunting a large enough private area the entire season. Deer become wise in a hurry if you use a particular stand more than a couple of times in succession. And with numerous stands, no matter what the wind direction, the weather, or the time of the season or rut, there will be always be

Bear River's ladder stand.

one tailored exactly to the prevailing conditions. (Though they last for many years, purchasing a dozen or more prefabricated stands is no small investment since they run from $75 to $175 a pop. A less expensive option is making your own, either through kits or blueprints available from ads in many of the archery magazines).

Hunting on public land can be more difficult, as there are often restrictions governing treestand use. In some areas, any stand left overnight becomes public property, which pretty much limits a hunter to one stand, set up for the day and then carried out after the evening hunt. A chain-on stand weighs twelve to fifteen pounds and is carried easily on a pack frame. In public lands which permit more than one stand, a chain-on offers the advantage of folding and padlocking when not in use, preventing theft or someone else sitting in your location. Screw-in tree steps are sometimes prohibited, but strap-on steps or a strap-on ladder serve just as well.

CLOTHING

I once made a wager with a man that I could kill a deer with a bow while wearing a white tuxedo, complete with tails and top-hat. Fortunately for my dignity, he backed out of the bet before anything ridiculous occurred. But my thinking was— and still is—that selecting the perfect stand location allows you to get off an undetected shot no matter what your choice of clothing.

However, most of the time the set-up is not perfect. Deer approach from an unexpected direction, or the leaves have fallen and no cover remains, or a deer surprises you while you're still-hunting slowly through the woods. At these times, the camouflage clothing you wear will very likely determine whether or not you get a shot.

The ability of camo to hide you—sometimes right out in the open—lies in how well it breaks up your outline. The color plays a role, of course, if it matches the terrain where you're hunting, but there's more to it than that. Some of the modern camos have a very large pattern, with different densities of color, which makes them look three dimensional to a game animal.

Those who hunt in hardwoods after frost, whether from a treestand or the ground, can't live another deer season without Skyline's new Apparition pattern. It's well-named, because its ability to make a hunter vanish is almost spooky. Recently, I was leaning against a tree beside a dirt road waiting for a hunting companion to pick me up. I was standing in the bald

Skyline's Apparition pattern, ideal for hardwoods.

open, except for the tree, when a whitetail doe appeared. She nibbled on browse as she meandered toward me, and after a few minutes finally passed upwind at a measured three yards. As far as she was concerned, I was invisible, which, of course, suited me just fine.

Predator is another large-pattern camo, offered in four distinct colors in their basic pattern. One of them will hide a bowhunter at close range under almost any kind of terrain or cover as conditions change throughout the season. I've used two of Predator's camo colors extensively, green early in the season and gray after frost. Predator offers a white camo, too, for those areas with snow during hunting season. Their winter gear is warm and comfortable, important attributes since it's difficult to sit still on a stand if you're half frozen. It's available in any of their four color combinations.

I'm hard on clothes, climbing trees, crawling through briars and mud like a reptile, crossing streams with the grace of a tank. In spite of my abuse, I've found Predator's clothing to be well-designed and durable. It's not all that expensive either, especially considering the quality.

A place I've had good luck finding discount camo clothing is the Army surplus store. The woodland pattern usually available is not optimum for every situation, but it works pretty well. For youngsters who outgrow a set of camos almost every year, this source really makes dollars and sense.

The better camo patterns work because they appear three dimensional. One type of camo actually *is* three dimensional. In a variation of the military ghillie suit used by snipers, Rancho Safari has come out with a bowhunter's version called a Shaggie Suit. Its strips of overlapping burlap and cloth sewn to a long jacket obliterate a hunter's silhouette, even when there is no cover whatsoever. The suit is bulky and hot when the temperature creeps above the seventies, and makes shooting a bow a bit awkward at first. Such camo is a lost cause when

A Shaggie Suit has limited uses, but is unsurpassed at rendering a bowhunter invisible.

you're moving, such as stalking or still-hunting, for it constantly snags on brush and briars. But for invisibility it has no equal and is tailor-made for a blocker on a deer drive or for rattling antlers during the rut.

As important as hiding you, your clothing must also be quiet. Most of the camo patterns are available in a variety of fabrics and clothing styles. Avoid any made from a rip-stop nylon or polyester type of material or light canvas. Try on a shirt, if possible, then move your arms as if you were drawing a bow. If you can hear anything other than the very faintest of rustles, the material is too loud. If your clothing makes noise when you draw your bow, it doesn't matter if you're invisible, you still won't get a shot for the deer will hear it. For maximum silence, look for 100% cotton or a cotton and polyester blend, brushed or sueded. In colder weather, the fleece garments offer warmth and silence, and one of my favorites in this cloth is Skyline's Apparition pattern. L.L. Bean offers fleece clothing in Predator camo patterns.

For more than a century, the old standby for traditional hunters has been wool. Today, any combination of cold and wet demands wool, as well. There are many brands of wool available for bowhunters today, but I've found only two which stand up to the worst conditions. The first, available in camo, is made by Swandri of New Zealand. Their cloth is made of the finest wool available, tightly woven, then dipped in vats of hot water to pre-shrink it and tighten the weave even more. The result is wool clothing which is virtually waterproof. Dressed in Swandri camo, I once spent most of a day in blowing rain, which froze shortly after it fell, perhaps the worst possible conditions. By the time I headed for camp, my bow, arrows, and nose sported icicles. But thanks to the quality wool, I was still dry and consequently was still warm.

To determine if wool clothing can withstand water, look closely at the cloth. If you can see individual threads, the weave is too loose to protect you from a day of sleet. This is also true if you hold the cloth up to a light and light shines through. The final test is to blow through the cloth. If you feel a slight resistance, then you are holding a quality wool which will last for years. These Swandri garments are not cheap, but still cost less than some highly-touted wool of much lower quality. The only importer of which I am aware is Screaming Eagle.

If you prefer no camo pattern on your wool clothing, Filson outerwear holds up to the elements as well as Swandri. Their Double Mackinaw Cruiser is especially warm, and their vest, with pockets for binoculars, deer calls, and hands, may be the most versatile, useful garment I own. Try their dark green coat and pants for hunting in timber, their solid gray or gray and black check for use in a treestand. Filson clothing is available at specialty sporting goods stores.

Surprisingly, the Army Surplus store occasionally has wool clothing. I recently bought my teenage son a pair of pants and a vest, of German manufacture, made from a medium green wool of good quality and excellent price.

Fingerless ragg wool gloves must have been invented just for bowhunters, for they keep your hands warm in all but subzero temperatures and allow the use of a shooting glove or tab. Most bowhunters wear some type of rubber boot both to keep feet dry and reduce human scent left on the ground when walking. L.L. Bean's boots with rubber bottoms and leather uppers have long been the standard for outdoor footwear.

In recent years, a couple of innovations have been introduced to hunting clothing: cloth which reflects no ultraviolet light and charcoal impregnated scent-absorbing cloth. Both of these products may have some small value, I'm not sure, but I am certain that our time—and money—would be much better served concerning ourselves with scouting, wind direction, and being more meticulous about stand location.

BINOCULARS

Most hunters probably already own at least one pair of binoculars. Volumes have been written about binoculars over the years, but in case you're contemplating buying another pair let me add my two cents worth here.

First some nomenclature about the size of binoculars, let's say 8 X 35, for example. The first number gives the power or magnification of the glass, 8 in this illustration. The second number, 35, gives the size in millimeters of the front, or objective, lens. The larger this number the bigger the lens, the more light it admits, and the clearer and sharper the image. A word, too, about lens coatings. Virtually every manufacturer today coats the glass with non-reflective coatings, meaning more of the light available enters the binoculars and ultimately reaches your eye. The better glass is coated several times at the molecular level, or multi-coated. But simply the words "multi-coated" aren't good enough, for some manufacturers multi-coat one or two lenses and single-coat the rest. The magic words to look for when considering binoculars are "fully multi-coated," an exercise in semantics, perhaps, but one which makes a tremendous difference in your ability to see under marginal light conditions.

Bowhunters primarily need a convenient set of binoculars, small and light enough so a hunter will be comfortable carrying them at all times. They are useful for judging the size of a trophy as he approaches from a distance and deciding whether or not to shoot. They are invaluable for stalking because to have any prayer of a shot with a bow, you must see the deer before the deer sees you. When not in use, these binoculars ride unnoticed. These glasses should be no more than 8 power, for larger magnifications are difficult to hold steady with one hand. The small objective lens of pocket 8 X 20 or 8 X 25's admit relatively little light, rendering these glasses all but worthless in very low light conditions. If selecting the ideal pair of binoculars for a bowhunter, the best choice is 7 or 8 power with a 30 or 35 mm objective lens. This larger lens makes the binoculars larger and slightly heavier than the pocket models, but the trade-off is well worth it for the increased light-gathering during prime times early and late in the day.

Though smaller binoculars will see the most use by a bowhunter, a larger pair is useful for scouting. In this case maximum magnification and light gathering are the goal, with little thought to weight or bulk, so at least a 10 X 42 glass is a logical choice. A 10 X 50 or 10 X 56 size is even better, for the large objective lens admits as much light as your naked eye. This means you will still be able to see through the binoculars up

The 7 X 30 Swarovski binoculars on the left may be the perfect binoculars for bowhunters; light weight, sharp images, and easy focusing with one hand. The big 10 x 56 Zeiss binoculars on the right are excellent for scouting, especially under low-light conditions.

until the very last moment in the evening, a very useful tool for scouting an elusive trophy buck from a distance.

All binoculars are not created equal when it comes to design. They should be easy and quick to focus with one hand. The neck strap should be comfortable to wear for twelve hours at a time. If you wear glasses, make sure a particular model still gives you a full field of view. The protective lens covers should be convenient and well-designed for field use as well as travel. Check all of these features with a critical eye when considering a pair of binoculars, for you'll find a great disparity in both engineering and quality between manufacturers.

Minolta and Pentax offer good binoculars for a democratic price. But if you don't mind spending your kid's college money, Swarovski and Zeiss make by far the best glass no matter what the size or model. "You get what you pay for" goes the old saying and nowhere is this more true than when it comes to binocular engineering, coated lenses, and glass quality. From the top-end manufacturers, a roof prism binocular is about twice as expensive as the standard porro prism tanker binoculars, but the extra money is well spent for the much lighter, more compact design. Hoping my sons will get a college scholarship, my personal choice is a pair of 7 X 30 roof prism Swarovski's. These may well be the perfect binoculars for bowhunters: super sharp images, instantaneous focusing with one hand, and modest weight. All of which means I'm never in the woods without them.

CALLS

Deer calls begin, of course, with rattling antlers. If you have access to real antlers, select a fairly large pair, cut off the brow tines to save on smashed fingers, and drill a hole at the base of each to attach a carrying thong. The synthetic plastic antlers available in sporting goods stores and catalogs work fine, too, and no, they don't just rattle up plastic deer. Although my experience with them has been limited, the "rattling bags"

Rattling antlers with carrying thong.

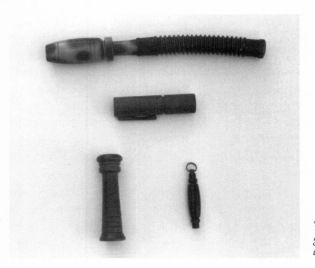

Two upper calls are grunts, two lower are fawn bleats.

filled with different sized dowel rods seem to attract deer as well as any other method. They're a whole lot more convenient to carry, too.

A bowhunter should never be without a grunt call which mimics the sound a buck makes when following a doe in heat, or a fawn bleat, which sounds like a fawn in distress. The section on Tactics contains an extensive discussion of how to use these calls.

SCOUTING

SCOUTING AT HOME

Though it may sound like wishful thinking, some of your most effective scouting will take place in your favorite recliner in the middle of your living room. Hard to believe, I know, but let's say you're hunting a new hotspot this season, a place out of state you've never seen. Let's further suppose that the land is a thousand acres of mixed hills, creekbottoms, and farmland. Before ever leaving home the topo map and aerial photo allow you to hunt not the entire thousand acres, but perhaps a half dozen of the very choicest two acre tracts where deer will be concentrated and the most vulnerable to a bowhunter.

It works like this.

A topo map's elevation lines show terrain features, and an aerial photo reveals vegetation. The more detailed and current these tools the better they'll serve you. For a place which will be hunted for several years, a useful refinement is to make copies of your topo map, then use a copy for each season. This way pertinent information about deer movement and scouting can be marked directly on the copy.

Deer spend most of their time in either bedding or feeding areas, and both can generally be pinpointed on the maps. In the old days, we always asked a rancher, "where's the thickest, nastiest place where no one ever goes?" and we'd have our bedding area. Look on the aerial photo for the thickest, darkest area of twenty to two hundred acres with no roads or other traffic. This is very likely a bedding area. Often, it lies in bottomland with solid trees and underbrush. It could be a swamp with dry islands or mounds. Sometimes, like here in Texas, a juniper-infested hillside is the bedding area. In such thick brush, bedded deer are almost invulnerable to stalking

Bedding areas are usually in the thickest cover available and can be pinpointed on an aerial photo. Did you see both bucks?

Agricultural fields are easily found on the aerial photo and are prime feeding areas, though once hunting season begins bucks such as this one seldom venture into them during daylight.

predators, two or four-legged. Pencil in likely bedding areas on the copy of the topo map. Mark them even if they lie outside your hunting area, for the activities surrounding you still profoundly affect deer movement where you're hunting.

Now for the feeding areas. In farming country, these are easy for deer love and depend upon crops such as alfalfa, corn, beans, oats, and wheat. Cropland on the aerial photo is an immediate prime suspect for a favored feeding area and should be marked on the map, even if they are on the property adjacent to your hunting land.

Let's suppose, to make it difficult, that there is no farmland on your photo. Deer still have preferred places to feed, principally areas which have been disturbed in some way. Disturbance, whether natural or man-made, fosters the growth of weeds (forbs) and second-growth brush (browse), both staples for deer. Such an area can be obvious on the photo; a clear-cut, a recent burn, a place where juniper or other brush has been bulldozed.

*Acorn-producing oaks
are sought out by the
deer and the wise
bowhunter should
follow suit.*

A feeding area's location might take a bit more detective work, usually obtained by questioning the landowner or manager (ask, too, about sightings of big bucks and other details about his deer herd, for his observations can be invaluable). When plants are still green and growing in the early fall, deer generally prefer to feed (but not bed) in a pasture out of which the cattle have recently been rotated. So ask about the location and rotation schedule of livestock. The cattle tend to disturb the ground with their hooves and eat down the grass, both of which help weeds to grow and browse to regenerate. Deer eat very little grass, it composes only about ten percent of their diet in the spring, and so don't complete with cattle for food unless the cattle are heavily overstocked.

Mast, or acorns and fruits such as persimmon, is the third major food group for deer. The prime feeding area might be several large white oaks, or a hillside of liveoaks, or a big buroak in a creekbottom, or persimmons with ripe fruit. If possible, landowners or someone familiar with the terrain should be questioned about the location and yield of oaks and other mast-producing trees.

A useful tidbit about oaks here in Texas; in October and November, when the acorns fall, deer sometimes congregate along dry, rocky creekbeds with overhanging oaks. The fallen acorns are much easier to find among the rocks and gravel of the streambed than among the leaves and brush along the banks, and these locations make prime ambush sites.

With the assistance of the aerial photo we've discovered the major bedding areas as well as likely favored feeding areas, and marked both on our copies of the topo map. Now all that remains is finding a deer funnel between the two. Any such funnel between a bedding and feeding area we'll mark on the map with a #1. A pronounced funnel standing alone we'll mark with a #2. In this way, we'll quickly narrow down the prime locations and secondary locations for a stand set-up. Again, mark them even if they are not on your property, for the more you

The author with the Pope and Young result of hunting funnels.

understand about deer movement on and around your place, the more effective you'll be.

Funnels are not a new concept—when I was a kid we used to call them "pinch-points." Everything, from a mouse to a musk ox uses them, even we humans. Consider your daily routine: driving from home to work and back again, dropping by the school, maybe a trip to the grocery store. We travel a particular route time after time largely for convenience, which is another way of saying we travel using funnels. And so it is with deer, though safety is far more important to them than convenience.

A deer funnel can be loosely defined as anything, natural or man-made, which causes game to travel in a restricted area. I've come to think in terms of negative funnels, which *prevent* game from traveling in a place, and positive funnels, which make game *want* to travel a particular path.

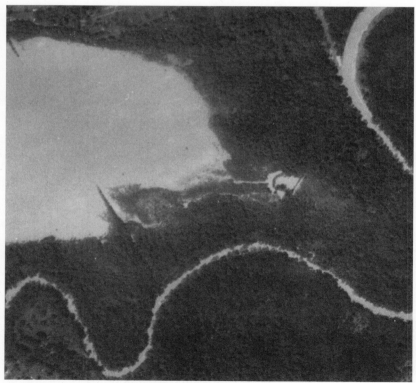

A lake forces deer to travel around it.

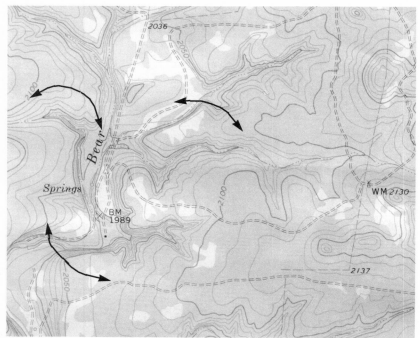

Cliffs such as these compress deer activity around each end.

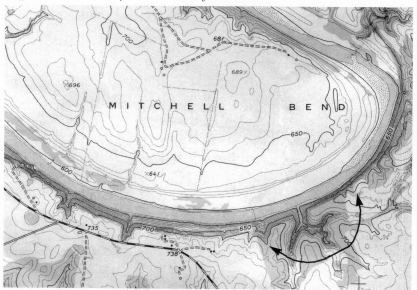

Another example of a cliff funnelling the deer movement.

An example of a negative funnel is a rock cliff that deer generally bypass. This will show clearly on the topo map; the closer the lines are together the steeper the cliff, which means that the deer trail will loop around one or both ends of the bluff, compressing the activity and making a likely ambush site. The longer the obstruction, the more this activity becomes compressed and the more deer use the trail. If this funnel lies between a bedding and a feeding area, mark the map with a #1 as a choice location for a stand.

A shallow crossing between two deep holes of water is an excellent funnel.

A lake or deep area of a river or creek is another obstruction which forces game movement around its ends. Such a barricade may be fifty yards or fifty miles long. Again, the longer and more impassable the blockage, the more the activity flows around it through the funnel. In some instances two obstructions create an excellent funnel between them that is almost guaranteed to be well-traveled, such as a saddle between two mountains or a shallow crossing between two deep holes in a river, both of which will show on the topo map. If this spot lies between a well-defined bedding and feeding area, mark it carefully on your copy of the map with a #1. If not, mark it with a #2 as a secondary spot.

Besides negative funnels, or obstructions, there are also positive funnels through which deer travel because they feel secure. Remember that deer, and especially the big guys, prefer remaining concealed in cover, so areas of thick brush in more open country are natural funnels and lanes of travel.

The more the deer are concentrated from a large area into a small one, the better the funnel. One of my aerial photos shows a place near a ranch that I hunt where one thickly wooded section connects with another only at one corner, like two dark squares on a chess board, with the surrounding areas open prairie. Though I've never actually been there, I'll start shooting a compound crossbow with a laser sight if there isn't a whitetail interstate highway where they connect.

Thickly wooded river bottoms of the western states are prime examples of positive funnels. An open bench often parallels the Blackfoot River in Montana, but between the base of this bench and the river, a distance ranging from thirty yards to three hundred, lies a stretch of timber so thick that in some places it looks like Cambodian jungle. The deer trails within this protected belt are awe-inspiring in size and perfectly suited for bowhunting.

But a funnel of this type doesn't always have to resemble rainforest to be extensively used, it just has to offer more cover than the surroundings. I once deerhunted a ranch which looked more like antelope country; rolling grassland dotted with cactus and mesquite, with infrequent motts of gnarled trees along the dry watercourses. Though the country seemed remarkably open, I arrowed a nice buck from the center of a clump of oaks

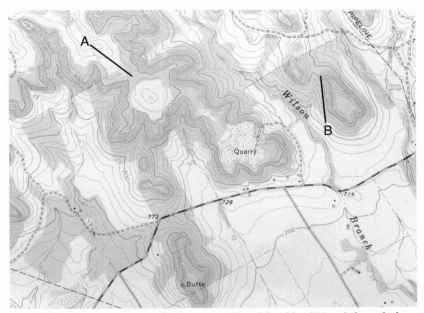

Deer will tend to move across the narrow section of the ridge (A) and through the saddle between the hills (B).

The narrow woods between the larger blocks of cover will see the greatest deer activity.

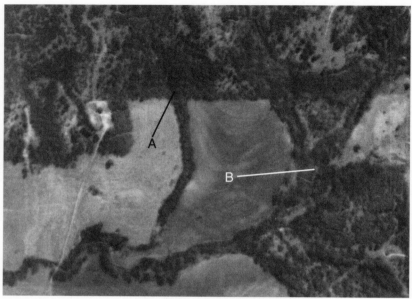

A T-funnel (A) covers two travel lanes, one just inside the edge of the cover, parallel to the opening, and the other into and out of the narrow stretch of woods. A classic funnel (B) forces deer from a wide area into a narrow one.

A "Y" funnel, a #1 location for a treestand.

as he traveled along low ground through the thickest part of the widely scattered trees.

Any site which combines more than one funnel can also be marked with a #1. In the Midwest, cropland interspersed with thick woods commonly occurs, and funnels abound. A ribbon of trees and brush which connects with a larger block of woods I think of as a T funnel. These should be marked as a #1, for you can cover two distinct travel patterns from one stand, one into the narrow travel lane and another along the edge of the woods. Narrow stretches of timber between corn fields are classic funnels. Where these narrow travel lanes split, or Y, should be marked with a #1, as well.

Low ground can serve as a funnel as it allows the deer to stay concealed, especially if they are heavily hunted. Where rifle season sounds like the Battle of the Bulge, deer like traveling—especially crossing a fence—in a depression or at the bottom of a hill, where they can't be seen from far away. These areas should show on the topo map. A brush-filled ditch or low place crossing an open pasture or crop field can also be heavily traveled.

Fences often appear as a dashed red line on the map, if not, they should be precisely drawn. If you suspect deer are moving through an area, and the only funnel you can find is a dip in the terrain along a fence, then you can mark it with a #2. If other funnel factors exist in conjunction with this feature such as heavy brush or a steep slope perpendicular to the fence, then the site rates a #1.

Consider a flat five hundred acre pasture with similar brushy vegetation evenly spread across it. No funnels, right? Not in the exaggerated sense of a cliff or a river, but as the deer move into, out of, and across the pasture they tend to travel along the fence. Hunting close to it greatly increases your chances over randomly picking a spot. If you can also find where deer leap the fence in a low place in the terrain you've doubled your odds in this difficult bowhunting country. Exactly this situation exists on a liveoak and juniper covered parcel in Central Texas where I frequently hunt. At a selected stand, about half the activity is along the fence and the other half back and forth over it, so as a result of this funnel I watch

Larger, wiser bucks will seek out the low ground, where they can't be seen from far away.

Deer cross this fence at the dip in the terrain.

a lot of deer through squinted eyes from fifteen yards away.

Another example of a fence funnel is an L corner, where deer can simply travel around the fence instead of having to jump it twice. I always note any L corners on a map, and look closely for other supporting funnels that would bump it up to a #1. The corner of a field or pasture poking into heavy woods also forms an L funnel. Deer tend to stay within the woods and avoid the opening, compressing their activity right at the bend.

A #1 location can be a funnel within a funnel: deer may be traveling through a stretch of thick timber, but if a low area lies within the brush, chances are the bucks prefer using it. Two and sometimes even three funnels can be found at one location: a rock cliff angling down to heavy timber along a river, a fence crossing a depression in the terrain within a peninsula of brush, a thickly wooded strip between a lake and a corn field. Mark any such multiple funnels with a #1, whether it lies between bedding and feeding areas or not.

By the time you've finished scouting at home, you may have marked a dozen or more prime #1 locations for stands, and have a fairly accurate idea of what the deer are doing, where they are traveling, and why. Making a real science of interpreting the maps lets you accomplish all of this without ever laying eyes on the property.

You say you've hunted the same place for thirty years and know it like the back of your hand? That you don't need a map to find deer? Maybe. But the aerial photo and topo map will be of even more value to someone intimately familiar with a place, for then the bedding and feeding areas can be pinpointed precisely. The invariable unsuspected funnels, the subtle places big bucks use, will quickly reveal themselves. You'll be astonished how often you refer to the maps and how instructive they can be—big buck sightings and deer patterns which never quite made sense before become crystal clear once the entire picture is laid out in front of you.

Everything else being equal, a fence tends to compress deer activity along it.

A fence crossing in some type of funnel is usually relatively easy to find and makes a prime ambush site.

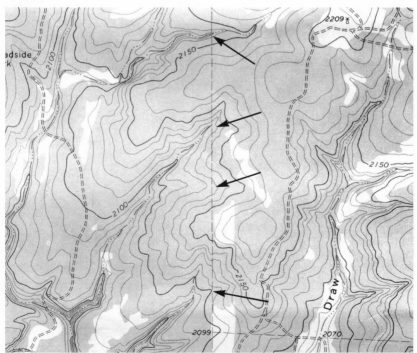

Such travel lanes and fence crossings at low places are easily seen on a topo map. Even the very subtle ones, such as the one at the bottom, are often heavily used.

53

Deer generally loop around an L-corner in a fence.

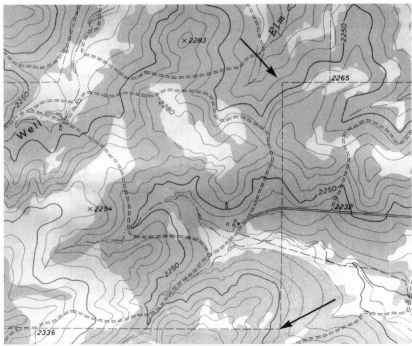

L-corners on a topo map.

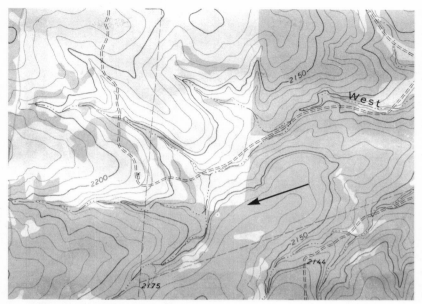

An open area can also make an L-corner.

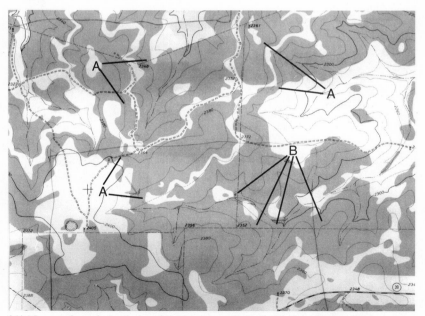

(A) Narrow funnels in timber. (B) Narrow spots in the timber along a fence.

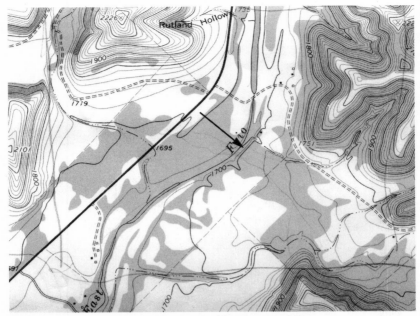

Double funnel. Strip of timber crossing ford between two lakes.

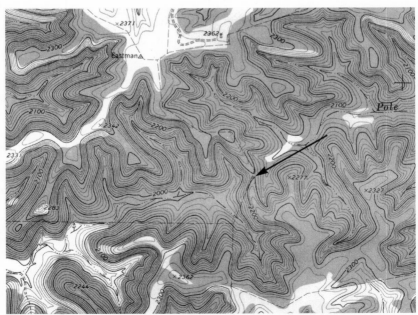

Double funnel. L-corner of fence located at saddle between hills.

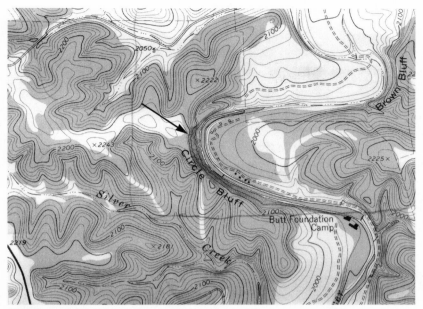

Double funnel. Narrow section of timber along cliff.

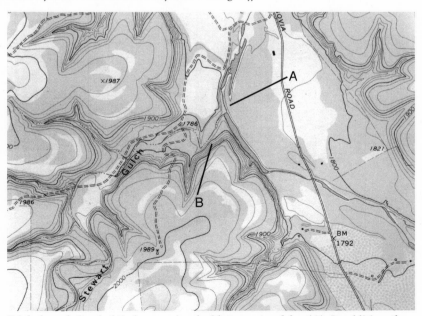

Triple funnel. Band of timber crossing ford between two lakes (A). In addition, the steep slope (B) tends to concentrate deer activity across the ford.

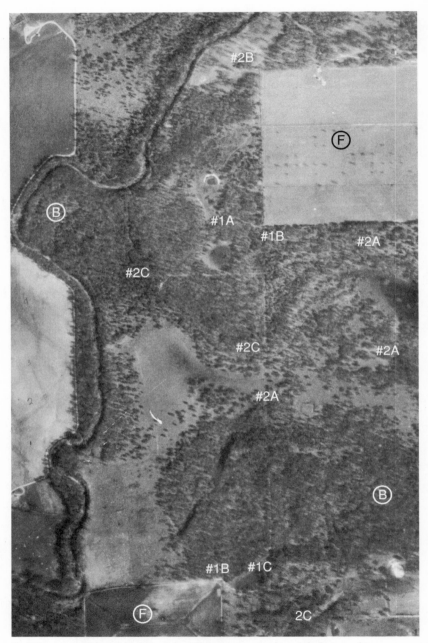

Bedding areas (B) and feeding areas (F) located on both aerial photo and topo map.
#1, funnels between bedding and feeding areas. #2, other funnels.

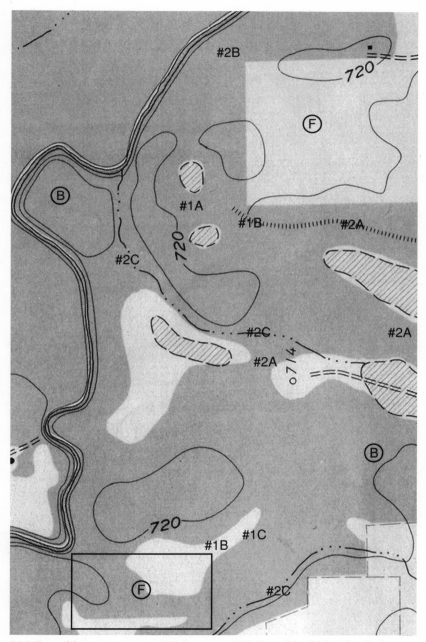

#1A-Funnel between swamps; #1B-L-corner; #1C-Funnel in thickest band of timber; #2A-Narrow area between swamps; #2B-L-corner; #2C-travel lane in low area.

SCOUTING IN THE FIELD

As we have seen, maps are invaluable for narrowing the search for deer. Actual scouting in the field, however, greatly fine-tunes the spots already chosen and adds a few more.

For the southern part of the country which has no winter-long snow cover, I've found the best time to scout to be immediately after the season. At this time you can relax and focus on deer sign and deer movement and not worry about the stealth of hunting. Rubs and scrapes remain relatively fresh and easy to spot. Too, the hunting pressure has left deer wary and much more nocturnal, so it's useful to jump deer on purpose in their bedding areas or sanctuaries to discover where they vanished when all the shooting started.

Up north, you can learn a great deal from tracking on snow before deer "yard up" during the depths of winter. One day of scouting on fresh snow is usually more revealing than a month of tracking on dry leaves and rock. After the snow melts in the spring is also a great time to scout, for rubs and scrapes are still

Snow can help pinpoint deer travel patterns.

Hunting shed antlers is an enjoyable excuse to be afield scouting after deer season.

evident, and shed antlers become easier to find. Shed hunting is fun in itself, but also can tell you where a mature deer survived hunting season, important information in planning next fall's strategy.

Early winter scouting reveals the deer's patterns during and after the rut, and late summer scouting previews what the deer will be doing when bow season opens. But you should try to spend time afield year round, for then you can keep track of acorn development, the fawn crop, planting and rotation of deer food crops, rainfall and its stimulation of weed growth, and a hundred other details which affect the lives of deer. Many of these factors will change by fall, naturally, but the more time you spend studying deer, their habitat, and their preferred foods, the better you understand their patterns and the more effective you'll be during hunting season. Successful

Shed antlers can be a great clue in finding a mature buck. These eight-point sheds, figuring a conservative 16" inside spread, scored 138". Any serious bowhunter, knowing the buck will likely be considerable larger the following season, will make a concerted effort to scout and set up on this deer.

bowhunters spend more time scouting in the off-season than they actually spend hunting in the fall.

If hunting a spot for the first time, first check the #1's marked on your map. You'll want to look for corroborating evidence that the deer are indeed using them; trails through the funnels, buck rubs, well-used fence crossings, beds, or droppings. Concentrated deer activity should be fairly obvious to the careful observer. Maybe half of the #1's will be disappointing for one reason or another. The brush was not as thick as it appeared on the photo, the crop field was left fallow this year, the deer didn't seem to travel through the saddle in the hills. I once found an ideal location on the map, several funnels pointing to a fence crossing. It was perfect. But actual examination revealed little use by the deer, for the ground was littered with softball-sized rocks, making jumping the fence treacherous. A nearby secondary funnel along the fence, to which I had given little consideration previously, consequently proved to be very heavily traveled.

A well-traveled trail through a funnel.

Erase any #1's which, for whatever reason, don't pan out. But if you've used the maps carefully, at least half of the sites will glow with promise. Recently, in late summer, I spent a couple of days poring over maps of a ranch I had never before hunted. I recorded about twenty ideal #1 spots. Upon arrival at the property, the rancher and I used four-wheelers to quickly examine the locations I had marked. We covered most of three thousand acres in two days, and placed an even dozen stands. The ranch owner seemed surprised that I could know exactly where his deer would be the first time I set foot on the property.

Find the funnels and you'll find the deer.

Later, from those stands, another hunter and I took nice Pope and Young bucks and a third missed a ten-point in the 150 inch range. There is no magic to this success, for the maps, along with careful scouting in the field, can put you on deer in a hurry.

Sometimes, if hunting a place for the first time, you're forced to scout as you hunt. This is the worst time, but you can still check your #1 locations as unobtrusively as possible and place stands where the sign warrants. Ideally, though, you're scouting at least a month before you plan to hunt so that you can do a thorough job without worrying about spooking deer. After checking the #1 locations on your map, search for other prominent deer signs. Without a great deal of experience, deer beds, tracks, and droppings are easy to misinterpret when scouting. With rubs, however, there can be no mistake. You KNOW they were made by bucks. And you can tell a lot about a buck from the rub he leaves when sparring and exercising with brush as the rut approaches. Though we've all probably witnessed exceptions, for the most part only big, mature bucks

Steven Hale with a fine Kansas buck taken at a pronounced funnel between a bedding and feeding area.

65

A rub can reveal a great deal about the buck which made it.

rub their antlers on big trees. They rub on smaller trees the size of your thumb too, of course, but if you find a tree three to six inches in diameter whose bark has been shredded by a buck, chances are he was a mature one, which usually means one with large antlers. You can also usually tell which way a buck was traveling when he stopped to make the rub. If you stand directly in front of the rubbed portion of the tree, you are facing the same way the deer was going when he paused.

On your copy of the topo map, every fresh rub you discover when scouting should be marked with a small x in a consistent color, such as red. A small arrow beside the x can indicate the buck's direction of travel. Big rubs which you suspect were made by a mature deer can be distinguished by circling the x (mark only fresh rubs because the completed copies of the topo maps for each successive year will all yield a slightly different, and revealing, picture). In the field, if you consciously look for rubs you'll find them. Along a deer's line of travel, you'll soon be able to predict where the next rub should be, because with the help of the maps you'll have a good idea where the deer came from and where he was going. Bucks usually like to travel in timbered bottomlands, just inside the edges of woodlots, and just below the crest of a ridge.

Travel lanes thus revealed by rubs can be useful, but I've become much more interested in groups of rubs because of the hunting success they've given me over the years. A group of rubs, up to a dozen or more in an acre or so, reveal an area

Recording rubs on the map can allow you to unravel the patterns of a particular buck.

where bucks spend a great deal of time. These multiple rubs fall into two basic categories.

One is found near a prime food source. Bucks, especially the bigger bucks, know they're vulnerable near a crop field, feeder, or open area of oak trees loaded with acorns. They rarely approach such a place until after dark, particularly after they've begun to feel the disruptions which hunting season brings (I know, I've also seen bucks that are lightly or never hunted walk out into cropfields in broad daylight like cattle. And during the rut they sometimes enter such an area checking for does in heat. But big deer which are hunter-smart rarely approach this type of place until after dark). So, the bucks usually wait near the food source in what have become known as "staging areas." I'm not sure who coined the phrase, but it's a good one. While waiting for darkness, the bucks congregate there, testing for weakness while sparring with each other and rubbing on nearby brush and saplings both to exercise and show off for the does. If you've ever watched a group of young teenage boys interact in the presence of girls, pushing, milling about, picking on each other constantly, then you know how bucks behave just before and during the rut. These staging areas are almost always found in thick cover and usually downwind from the food source from fifty to a hundred yards. Ideally, you should find where deer are entering the area. Mark this spot on your map with a #1, or maybe two #1's. As long as the food lasts it will be a prime spot in the fall.

The second category of rubs is more difficult to find, though discovering one is even more valuable than a staging area. Most hunters have had the experience of seeing big bucks early in the season or before the season begins, never to see them again. It's almost as if they've been vaporized or swallowed up by the earth. But they haven't, for spotlight counts around food sources invariably disclose bucks far bigger than most hunters are seeing. When scouting, if you happen through an out-of-the-way place where no one ever goes, if the brush is thick but the overall area small, and if you find several rubs on larger trees, then you've probably discovered where a mature buck vanishes each fall. More about these sanctuaries and how to predict where they'll be in the section on Hunting the Big Guys,

Staging areas, revealed by rub concentrations, near a wheatfield.

but mark the spot on your map with a #1 and save it like gold for the next season.

Scrapes, where bucks have pawed the ground then urinated, should be marked on the map in a different color. These scrapes will vary widely depending upon what part of the country you hunt. On some ranches, I've seen scrapes the size of a kitchen table, while on others I've seldom found one bigger than a hat. This difference is largely due to the buck-to-doe ratio, since bucks use these scrapes to locate does in heat. Maybe northern and southern species of deer are different enough to explain some disparities. Likely the drawn-out rut of southern deer as opposed to the more sharply defined rut of those in the north is also part of the explanation.

A dominant buck making a scrape.

No matter where you hunt, these scrapes can be a valuable clue in finding bucks, and especially big bucks. Look for scrapes under the low-hanging branches of a tree along travel corridors, in funnels, and along the edges of cropfields and woodlots. They'll often be in a line, much like rubs in a travel lane. The pawed area on the ground should be relatively easy to see but the sure sign of a bona-fide scrape location is the chewed and frayed twigs hanging four feet or so above the pawed ground. Scrapes are easiest to find in the south immediately after the season or in the north as soon as the snow melts in spring. Some hunters, such as Gene Wensel of Montana and Roger Rothhaar of Ohio, have specialized in hunting scrapes. They make mock scrapes or treat scrapes with commercial scents and have developed this style of hunting into a fine art. If you hunt an area with heavy scraping activity, indicate large scrapes with a distinctive color on the map. Plan to set a stand fifty yards downwind (bucks often scent-check a scrape from a distance without approaching) and use it just as the rut begins.

Clint Thomas with a bruiser of a Kansas buck taken near a scrape.

Another result of scouting will be actual big buck sightings. Late summer or early fall locations should be marked lightly on the map, for he will likely alter his movements somewhat as hunting season approaches due to cooler weather and changing foods. Sightings immediately prior to or during the season can be valuable information, however, and should be noted on the map. Stands already placed where he's been seen should receive special attention, and funnels previously discounted in his area should get another look. At times, a good buck will be repeatedly seen where you wouldn't expect it. Don't argue with the deer. He has perfectly good reasons for his actions, and if you catch him doing something more than once and don't spook him chances are he does it all the time. The maps can help you plot a way to move into his area and set up on him.

If you see a nice buck, try to get a look at his tracks, if you can do so without alerting him. Often, a large buck's tracks are distinctive as to size or features such as very blunt tips or one toe shorter than another. Such individual characteristics can allow you to recognize the track in the future. Tracks can be

marked on the map to help further unravel a particular deer's pattern.

Off-season scouting quickly confirms bedding areas. If the livestock are non-existent or moderately stocked the resulting tall grass readily shows where it has been depressed. Matted leaves and forest litter are often just as easily read. If you jump a deer from its bed, always examine where he was lying. Note which way he was facing and what he could see. Consider wind direction and how he used it to detect approaching trouble. Was the weather a factor? Did the bed help protect the deer from wind or precipitation? Ask these questions and more, and the bedding habits of deer will soon become predictable. Mark those beds which, because of their size or location in an especially hard to approach place, indicate they might have been made by a buck.

You can bet this buck chose his bed with security high on his list.

Up until now, all of the funnels discussed have been natural, but there remains one further refinement which should be noted. The way we use a series of stands can influence deer movement and create funnels. Permanent stands, whether on your property or adjoining places, should be marked. Through research with radio telemetry, Dr. James Kroll has proven that

Carefully examining beds and understanding why they were chosen allows the bowhunter to predict where bedding areas will be.

deer, especially larger bucks, quickly become wise to permanent blinds and tend to avoid them. True, hundreds of trophy deer are taken with rifles from just such stands every year, but I'm convinced that many thousands more big bucks are wise enough to avoid such obvious danger and are NOT taken. By noting where these stands are located, you can often determine how the deer sidestep them and plan your strategy accordingly.

Recently, I sat in a treestand we refer to as "Old Reliable." It had undoubtedly become a little TOO reliable, since I watched a nice buck circle the stand just out of range, occasionally glancing toward my tree, and jump a fence onto another property. Examination of his fence crossing revealed that he had traveled within twenty yards of a long shooting lane cleared from a permanent box blind. The hunter sitting in the blind never saw the deer, who had neatly and calmly sidestepped both a bowhunter and rifle hunter in one move. Any portable stand which is used repeatedly over several years can suffer the same burnout as a permanent stand and affect deer movement. Several times I've had the humbling experience of sitting in a treestand I considered well-placed, only to have deer peek around a bush fifty yards away and peer directly into my tree, to see if anyone was sitting in the stand that day. It's no accident that when a big buck is killed it's often from a stand which was being used for the first time.

Another man-made funnel is one, as far as I know, about which Gene Wensel first wrote. I've used this trick dozens of times and it bears repeating here. By tying down the top two wires of a fence, and making it easier to jump, you can encourage deer to cross in a particular place. In my experience, tying

Tying down a fence accentuates an existing crossing.

Big bucks can also go under fences.

down the fence is much more effective at accentuating an existing crossing the deer already use than trying to create a crossing where none existed. Anytime I place a stand at a fence crossing now I automatically tie down the fence because it helps compress deer activity. It works equally well to tie the bottom two wires up at a low place. Don't worry about bucks getting their antlers under the wire, for they can scoot through a place that might look as though it would turn a rabbit. Of course, consult with the landowner—or *be* the landowner— before laying a finger on a fence. In a similar vein, you can drop a tree to block a trail and force the deer to move nearer a perfect set-up for a stand.

One last refinement with the maps. Throughout the year, I like to note on the back of the map a thumbnail sketch of environmental patterns such as rainfall, drought, acorn yield, crops, etc. Details of the kills should also be noted: numbers, age, sex, and size of bucks. Thereafter, you have a concise record of the year's activities, and after three or four years the correlation between environmental factors and deer movements will allow you to more accurately predict future activity. For example, a lack of sufficient rainfall during the summer might mean the rut will be less distinct and more drawn out than normal in the fall. Or a bumper crop of acorns will translate into less deer activity around food plots. The more information you have about your deer and their past, the more effective you'll be as their predator.

STAND PLACEMENT

After scouting, you now know which funnels and fence crossings are heavily used. You know staging areas and travel lanes from the rubs. You've pinpointed bedding and feeding areas. At least half the battle is won at this point, for you've determined where the deer will be. The other half of the battle is setting up on them where they can't detect you.

When locating a sight for a stand, the first consideration is always wind direction. A deer's nose is his most impregnable defense, and I'm convinced that more deer are alerted to a hunter's presence by scent than by all other factors combined. The worst part is that the hunter usually remains blissfully unaware that his odor has given him away; the deer simply fail to appear.

A steady wind is best for a hunter, for a very faint, fickle breeze which changes and eddies will almost certainly alert the deer by permeating the area with your scent. For flat calm days you can place a stand in relation to the morning and evening thermals, which are highly predictable. In the mornings, the rising sun warms the air and tends to make it move uphill; in the evenings the air cools and tends to flow downhill, like water. The most desirable condition is a modest, steady breeze, followed by calm conditions with its thermals, and finally a slight, swirling breeze. In fact, many hunters will not sit a stand when the wind is not steady, for doing so simply contaminates the area for future use. If the wind changes or is not what I expected while on a stand, I'll usually climb down and try stalking or horn rattling elsewhere to prevent ruining the site. A wind feather is invaluable in these situations for determining what the wind is actually doing.

Fortunately, deer don't just travel into the wind, for if they did we'd never kill one. Since deer play the odds they usually seem more reluctant to move with the wind directly at their

Any bowhunter who underestimates a deer's nose is guaranteed an empty freezer.

backs when they would be most vulnerable to a predator lying in wait. Even when they do move with the wind, does or small bucks are likely to catch your odor after they've passed and give the alarm by bolting or snorting. Therefore, the ideal setup is a cross-wind situation with the stand on the downwind side of the trail, so deer will be comfortable moving but will be unlikely to catch a hunter's scent.

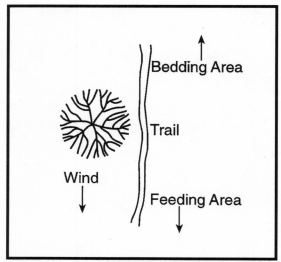

If simply after a deer, this set-up works fine for an evening stand. If the hunter is selective and wants a buck, however, does and yearlings will pass by first and likely wind the hunter and alert the other deer.

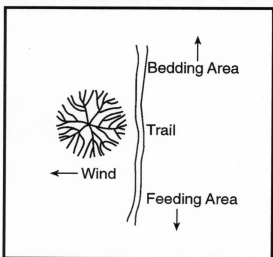

The ideal set-up. Deer are more comfortable moving in a cross-wind situation and does and yearlings can't detect the hunter or reveal his position.

With this in mind, select a tree ten to fifteen yards from the trail or fence crossing. In several of my better deer funnels, I place two stands, one for a south wind and one for a northwest wind, the two primary directions in the Texas Hill Country during hunting season. Usually, you can select a tree in relation to the prevailing wind. Sometimes though, the set-up will be such that there is only one tree in which you can place a stand,

and that stand will only be usable when the wind is out of a particular direction. In a prime location, I always go ahead and hang such a stand, because multiple locations for several different wind scenarios are highly desirable for then I always have a place to hunt no matter what the conditions.

While we're on the subject of wind and scent, most hunters know to eliminate strong odors as much as possible. Don't pump gas while wearing your camos. Change hunting clothes before the evening's meal to avoid the odors of campfire smoke or frying onions. Don't smoke tobacco or shower with scented soap. While in hunting camp, hang camo clothing outdoors in dry weather, or keep the clothing in a garment bag along with cedar or sage or some other local plant. All simple, basic precautions which help eliminate odor.

In a borderline situation, where a few molecules of human smell have drifted to a deer, a cover scent may help you remain hidden or make a deer think you're much farther away. Though some dislike skunk scent because it broadcasts the fact that something alarmed a skunk, I've not found it to bother deer and have, on numerous occasions, had them pass downwind

Spraying a cover scent on boots and legs helps mask a hunter's trail into and out of a stand.

without detecting me. A plastic film canister filled with cotton balls works great for containing the ever-volatile skunk essence; just uncap it when on the stand, then cover it up and replace it in a pocket when ready to leave. My favorite cover scent for hunting in Texas is juniper oil mixed with water. With a spray bottle the scent can be applied to legs and bootsoles, which not only gives a subtle cover odor but helps mask your trail into the stand, as big a tip-off to the deer as a direct whiff of you when you're sitting in a stand. Since using the juniper scent, I can't recall a deer ever spooking upon crossing my trail, as they often did when no such precaution was taken. Now, deer sometimes notice the trail where I've walked to the stand, but seem only curious and after a few moment's inspection flick their tail and continue casually on their way. I highly recommend some local cover scent sprayed on boots and legs to reduce the deer's awareness of your presence. You can make your own by gathering a local strong-smelling plant such as pine, sage, or cedar, bruising the leaves lightly with a hammer, then boiling them or placing them in the sun in a covered water-filled jar, like making sun tea. The commercial scents are easier and more concentrated but home-made concoctions insure a local scent to which the deer are accustomed.

While odor control on our clothing and cover scents undoubtedly help, I'm certain that all the cover scents in the world are worthless if a stand is set wrong or the wind swirls too much. We are always better served being meticulous about stand selection in relation to the wind than relying on some magic potion to render us invisible to a deer's nose.

Attractor scents, such as doe-in-heat lures, have become increasingly popular in recent years. After trying many of them I can only report that the results have been mixed, at best. I've finally decided that rather than attempting to completely fool a buck's most powerful and least understood defense, his nose, that it is far more effective to pinpoint what the deer are doing naturally and catch them doing it.

In any case, if you have time before season, the deer's movement through a funnel can be precisely pinpointed by watching from a distance. This is where a big pair of binoculars pays for themselves by allowing viewing very early and very late. You must be certain that your presence won't alert the deer, but such scouting can tell you exactly in which tree a stand should be placed.

Deer never look up. Yeah, right.

Once a particular tree or group of trees is selected for a stand cover must be considered in addition to the wind, for I'm convinced deer see movement even better than we do. Try to

Back to the deer as they approach.

The shot is made after the deer has passed and is quartering away.

place a stand where there is plenty of background foliage to help break up your silhouette. The stand should be set so that the hunter's back is to the deer as they approach. For right-handed shooters, the animal should pass by on the hunter's left. In this admittedly ideal situation, the hunter is hidden by the tree until the deer goes by, then the shot is made quartering away (While dreaming about the ideal stand, select a tree which places the morning or evening sun in the deer's eyes. When after animals who act as though they were born with a nervous breakdown, little nuances like this make the difference between getting shut out and neatly wrapped packages of venison in the freezer).

Install the screw-in tree steps for reaching the stand by screwing them into the tree until the side lies flush against the bark. A short length of 1" PVC pipe gives additional leverage and makes the job easier. I found out the hard way that screw-in steps should only be used in sturdy woods, never soft wood such as cottonwood or aspen. I was twenty feet up an aspen in Montana a couple of seasons ago, a snowy hour before

A short section of 1" pipe takes the work out of installing or removing screw-in tree steps.

One glance at the ears shows these deer are relaxed. The perfect shot quartering away.

daylight, when a step I was standing on pulled completely out of the tree, causing my other foot to slip from its step. Dangling in the darkness, I clung desperately with one hand, for, oh, about a decade, until finally locating another step with one foot. You may be assured that I came down from that treestand a couple of hours later very gingerly.

Once a tree is chosen, how high should you place the stand? In general, twelve to fifteen feet is high enough to be less noticeable to deer, while anything over twenty feet is too high. Preferable to shooting straight down from a skyscraper stand, a side shot from a modestly placed one offers a larger target. An arrow from the side also increases the chances of piercing both lungs and achieving complete penetration which makes tracking and recovery much easier. Twelve to fifteen feet to the bottom of the stand is about right for most situations. In trees

Two shooting lanes 90 degrees apart in the same tree. Note how back cover helps hide the hunter's silhouette.

with little cover, such as big pines or cottonwoods, set the stand higher to remain undetected. In liveoaks whose gnarly, crooked trunks are usually unsuited for a chain-on stand, one of the folding fork stands can be placed fairly low, eight or ten feet, if you choose the tree carefully.

Sometimes, the most difficult part of the hunt lies in drawing an arrow after closing within ten or fifteen yards of a deer. Though they are somewhat less attuned to danger from above, this in no way implies they are oblivious to it. In fact, deer which are heavily bowhunted from treestands often walk through the woods looking up at trees like dedicated bird watchers. If you sit in plain view, the telltale movement of drawing a bow can blow an otherwise perfect setup. Evergreen trees such as cedar, pine, or liveoak offer the best cover, especially after frost when most other leaves have fallen. I prefer setting up in a tree with fairly thick foliage for the cover, then cutting shooting lanes, narrow clearings a couple of feet wide cleared through the limbs of a tree which allow passage of an arrow. You can begin the draw while the deer is still behind

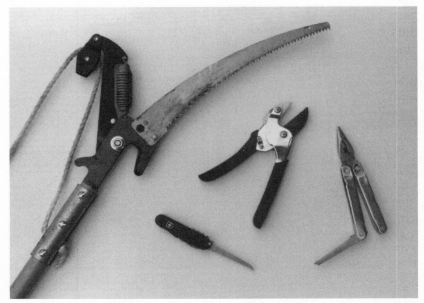

A pole saw is essential for trimming hard to reach branches in a shooting lane. Hand clippers and a small saw on a Leatherman tool or Swiss Army Knife are handy, too.

the cover, then anchor and release as he steps into the open. I like to prepare two or three such lanes, usually one to the left, one straight ahead, and one to the right, in case deer forget to read the script and don't pass exactly where I'd planned.

Also, after setting the stand, carefully clear branches and leaves which might touch your bow and create noise from any shooting position, standing or sitting. Pruning shears and a small saw are convenient for this as well as for clearing shooting lanes. You'll find a pole saw, complete with a rope-operated branch trimmer, invaluable for cutting hard-to-reach limbs when you first set a stand. A locking-blade Swiss Army Knife, the one which includes a small saw blade, was apparently invented just for bowhunters since the saw is so handy for fine-tuning treestands. Be careful about leaving odor on trimmed limbs which fall to the ground; try not to handle them but use a stick to drag them well away from the trail.

After you've sat in a stand a time or two, you might notice that most of the deer activity is nearby but not quite close enough. Don't hesitate to unobtrusively move a stand based upon your observations in the field. By moving a stand to a better location then immediately entering it and sitting until dark, we often pull the rug out from under a buck who has no clue he's being hunted.

There will be times, either through circumstances or your own inclination, when you won't use a treestand. Ground blinds can be just as effective though the wind is more of a problem. I've had best success with a ground blind during the rut, when rattling antlers, or during a deer drive. These blinds can be as simple as kneeling behind a low-growing cedar or standing amid the trunks of a clump of liveoaks, using undisturbed natural features to hide your shape. Sitting in a ground blind is the time to wear your best camo such as a ghillie suit. If possible, the blind should be in the deep shade on a sunny day so your shape and movement of drawing a bow will be harder for the deer to see. A ground blind in direct sunlight should be saved for a cloudy day. The shot should be set up so that you are hidden until the deer is past, it is then easier to draw for the quartering away shot without him seeing the motion. Problems with wind are minimized if you can stand at

Thick clump of brush and low-growing trees...

...and the narrow shooting lane for an arrow.

a higher elevation than the deer. One of my best stands is a ground blind where a steep hill pinches down close to a creek, funneling the deer through a twenty yard opening. By standing amidst the brush up on the hillside, the shot is almost identical to a treestand shot, about 45 degrees downhill, quartering away.

A ground blind can be more elaborate. Brush can be stacked around existing trees or other brush to leave room for a seated hunter inside. The more you can use natural cover, and the more perfectly you can blend the blind into the surroundings, the better. All of this should be done well before season to allow deer to grow used to any disturbance. The same strategy applies here—have complete cover as the deer approaches then a shooting lane after the deer is past. A blind can be constructed like a turkey blind, with brush stacked high enough to conceal the upper limb of the bow and just a hat-sized hole to shoot through. A low seat or bucket makes the waiting more comfortable.

Another variation of a ground blind is a pit blind. Antelope hunters use these to hide in open country, and they can work

Charlie Davis and a fine buck taken from a ground blind.

just as well for whitetail hunters, especially in the western states where deer are much more comfortable in the open than those in the eastern forests. Big bucks regularly traverse sage-brush-covered benches on their daily rounds and are just as safe from the average stalking bowhunter as are the antelope. A pit blind, a hole about three feet deep with a seat for the hunter, can offer a shot in this very difficult terrain. Of course, any natural cover such as sagebrush or tall grass should be used to advantage. Also, the dirt from the hole is best stacked onto a piece of canvas and dragged some distance away down-wind. With the farmer's permission, a pit blind might be a strategy worth considering in an agricultural field, where the deer feel invulnerable from approaching predators.

Tripods are a very specialized form of stand, with a seat and footrest atop three legs which can be from six to fifteen feet tall.

A tripod is tailor-made for situations with no suitable tree for a treestand.

Fourteen-year-old Matt Davis and the results of hunting from a tripod - his first deer with a bow.

In most applications, some other type of stand will work better and be easier to set up, but for the low-growing brush and cactus found in much of the Texas deer habitat a tripod is a natural. Bowhunters in the so-called Brush Country of southern Texas which has a solid mass of thorny vegetation six to ten feet tall use tripods extensively. In this region, there is no place for a treestand and from a groundblind your visibility is generally about four feet. If you hunt a place with similar cover with no place for a treestand or groundblind, you might consider a tripod. In thick junipers as in much of the Southwest, a tripod is an excellent choice but there is another option, as well. Cut the trunk of a juniper about eight feet above the ground where the trunk is four inches in diameter and remove the top of the tree. One of the old metal tractor seats can be screwed into the flat base left where the trunk was cut. With judicious clearing, this set-up yields a treestand's advantages of giving an undetected shot in a place where no treestand can be placed.

Use your imagination when planning a stand in one of your #1 locations, but remember wind, cover, and shooting lanes. The total number of stands will vary depending upon the length of the season and the size of the area being hunted. But a hunter who just has one stand location won't kill many deer with a bow. The first evening on the stand he'll probably see numerous deer, the second evening a few, and from then on none. For a season lasting a month or more, every hunter needs at least a dozen stands so he'll have one for every wind condition and can let a stand "rest." I regularly hunt a seven hundred acre tract in the Texas Hill Country, where bowhunting lasts for three straight months, counting rifle season. On this place, I have a total of twenty-three stands: four ground blinds, fourteen treestands, three ladder stands, and a couple of tripods. I always have a prime place to hunt, no matter what the wind direction or time of the season.

THE PLAN

OVERALL STRATEGY

Most hunters hang a half-dozen stands in good spots and sit in them pretty much at random depending upon wind direction. At times they rattle antlers or try grunt calls. They see deer and may even have some success over the years and take a nice buck or two. These hunters may be meticulous about wind and stand selection, practice with their bow religiously throughout the summer and early fall, and have learned volumes about deer and deer behavior. But they're neglecting

Jim Welch is an observant and thoughtful hunter, always staying one step ahead of his quarry. Deer such as this South Dakota buck are the rewards for such care.

x

what I believe to be the most important aspect of consistently killing deer. If you take nothing else away from this book please take this—if hunting a single piece of property, you must have a cohesive, overall strategy for the entire season, for any other approach spooks the deer herd early and almost guarantees few, if any, shots.

A buck like this is no accident. David Sykes' strategy produced the Texas ten-point.

Deer are exquisitely sensitive to change and react to it by becoming more cautious and nocturnal. Deer can become accustomed to almost anything, it's the *change* which they distrust. I live on the far outskirts of a large metropolitan area and the local deer have learned to co-exist with man quite well. These deer, while wild and very difficult to hunt, think nothing of traffic, laughing children, low-flying jets, barking dogs, or many other activities which would initially send deer from a wilderness area into cardiac arrest. Make sure you don't tip off the deer you're hunting by giving them anything unusual to worry about.

When planning strategy to minimize the effects of your presence, consider the three phases of the season. Early in the

Deer are so adaptable they can get used to almost anything.

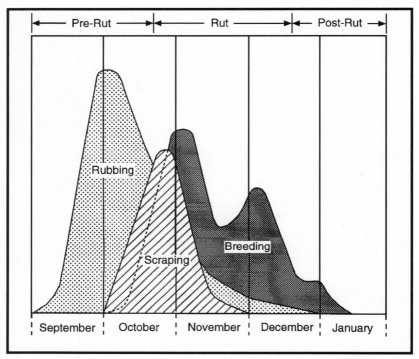

Strategy should be different for the pre-rut, rut, and post-rut. The overall timing and ratios of this chart are correct, but actual dates in your particular area may vary by several weeks.

fall, or in the pre-rut, the deer remain largely in their patterns from late summer, relaxed and pretty much set in a routine of traveling to feeding areas in late afternoon and returning to bedding areas after sunrise. As the rut approaches, the bucks become more and more pugnacious, exercising by rubbing their antlers on trees, sparring with each other, and making scrapes. When the first does go into heat, the Chinese firedrill of the rut begins, with bucks chasing does throughout the day, fighting with each other, or wandering about searching for does. After the rut ends, or in the post-rut, the bucks are exhausted, having sometimes lost up to twenty-five percent of their body weight during the breeding season. They are now interested primarily in eating and stocking up on fat reserves for the winter. They are also exceedingly cautious, with many becoming virtually nocturnal, for hunting season has been well

Determine exactly when the rut occurs in your area.

underway in most areas and the deer are on alert. This is when bucks seen earlier in the season seem to vanish.

The three phases—pre-rut, rut, and post-rut—often seem to overlap and blend to some extent, but overall strategy should be planned around them. Keep in mind that different parts of the country experience vastly different rutting activity. In Canada, Montana, and Minnesota, the rut is usually very sharp and distinct, lasting a frantic ten days or so in November then ending abruptly. In the southern states the rut is less clearly defined, sometimes beginning in mid-October—reaching a peak in mid to late November—then lasting until the first of the year or later. In some states, archery hunting lasts for months and encompasses all three phases of deer activity, in others the season lasts only a week during the peak of the rut. Even regions in close proximity can have the rut vary by several weeks, so you must determine, either through direct observation or reports from state game departments, exactly where your season falls during the three phases of activity.

In the pre-rut period early in the season, you want to hunt funnels and staging areas near food sources. You can often get the drop on the deer before they realize they're being hunted. In the mornings you'll have to select stands farther from the food source, so you can slip into them undetected while the deer are still feeding. Some stands will lend themselves to mornings, some to evenings, and some to both. As the rut approaches, rattling antlers, grunting, and hunting scrapes becomes more and more effective. Plan to regularly hunt all day when the rut arrives as the bucks constantly chase does. For the same reason, the rut is the time to hunt #2 funnels found between bedding areas, for the bucks travel between these places looking for does in heat. After the rut, hunt as close to bedding areas as you dare. Right at the end of the season is the time to conduct drives through bedding areas and sanctuaries.

In general, begin the fall hunting near food sources and as the season progresses incorporate rut tactics while working back toward bedding areas. If sightings drop off, move closer to

#2 funnel between bedding areas. Hunt these locations for the first time during the rut.

the bedding area. A simple plan for hunting a property the entire season, but very effective. It's surprising how many hunters never consider the long-term results of their actions and hunt near bedding areas from the very start, or begin staging deer drives after sitting stands a few times, or rattle antlers every day of the fall. All of these activities are guaranteed to spook deer early and force them into nocturnalism and a state of hyper-alertness, which means that they are all but invulnerable to a bowhunter. Plan your strategy for taking advantage of the deer's normal activity while disrupting that activity as little as possible.

There are some further tricks for preventing the deer from lying low. Instead of a hunting party spreading out to stands across an entire property—and alerting all the deer in the process—they should hunt one end of the place for a day or two, then switch to the other end where the deer are still unaware and relaxed. Don't use the same stand two days in a row, no matter how good it seems, unless the wind was perfect and you executed a bulletproof approach and exit. If possible, let it rest for at least three or four days before using it again.

While having such a well-laid strategy will greatly increase your chances for success, the operation should not be chiseled in marble. Like a football game plan which adapts as the contest unfolds, so should your plan adapt to the conditions you observe in the field. But before you make a new move, think long about how it will effect the deer both in the short term and for the remainder of the season. Such careful planning and the resulting overall flexible strategy may be the most underrated but effective weapon in the bowhunter's arsenal.

ENTERING AND LEAVING A STAND

How you approach and depart a stand is every bit as important as the actual stand location. Just as a human who has almost stepped on a rattlesnake will unconsciously look in that spot every time he passes, so will a deer who has gotten a strong whiff of you or your trail be extra cautious in that area. Years ago, a nice eight pointer unexpectedly approached my treestand on the downwind side. When he reached the tracks I had left well before daylight he screeched to a stop, sniffed the ground with a curl of his lip, then instantly reversed course and melted back into the brush. For the rest of the season, that particular buck was likely unkillable from that stand. A cover scent sprayed on legs and bootsoles, such as the juniper oil mixed with water mentioned earlier, helps minimize such a negative reaction from the deer. Rubber boots, or rubber-soled boots such as L.L. Bean's, leave much less man-scent than leather boots, especially when sprayed with such a cover scent.

Though as bowhunters we pride ourselves on our stealth, in truth bowhunting probably disturbs the deer's normal activities even more than rifle hunting. We are not sniping unsuspecting deer from another area code with a rifle, but sneaking about and setting up in a deer's living room at the "excuse me" ranges an arrow demands. An accomplished bowhunter never forgets this fact and constantly guards against putting the deer on alert.

Look on the maps and plan your route to the stand so as to cause the least disruption given the existing wind condition. Always approach a stand from downwind and never walk across or in the trail you expect deer to use. Those who regularly hunt in snow know that deer can go on alert just by *seeing* your tracks, not even counting scent, so take this into consideration when traveling the last thirty yards to a stand. A stand should be stalked, slowly, by pretending that a deer is bedded down under it, as might well be the case. Carefully plan your approach so that you don't disturb or travel upwind from bedding or feeding areas, depending upon where you expect the deer to be. You may have to travel far out of your way to accomplish this, maybe a mile or more. The exit route from a stand might have to be completely different, though just as far. All of this effort is well worthwhile, for hunting undisturbed deer is far easier than hunting deer who know a human predator lurks in the woods with them.

Many hunters make the mistake of driving within a couple hundred yards of their stand. If such vehicle movement is normal at that time and at that place, well and good. In fact, if the stand is near a road, having a companion quietly and quickly drop you off is a good strategy for limiting disturbance and scent. If, however, the movement of a four-wheeler, jeep or

Hunters who drive close to their stands are greatly appreciated by the deer.

other vehicle is NOT normal in that location, then you might as well be leading a brass band when you drive close to your stand and park.

Reaching a stand in thick woods in the pitch dark sometimes presses woodcraft to the limit and beyond. This is especially true if you want to be truly benevolent and allow a friend to sit one of your prime locations and he's never been there before. Cat's Eyes, or thumbtacks with a reflective material on the head, are the answer to the problem and I now place them on all of my morning stands. A tack placed in a tree every ten or fifteen yards allow a flashlight-carrying hunter to easily and quietly follow his trail to the stand. Place three Cat's Eyes in a triangular shape on the tree which actually holds the stand.

Planning a discreet entrance and exit from your stands cannot be overemphasized. Some stands may be situated so that they can only be used a couple of times before the deer figure you out, while if you're careful others can be used throughout the season and the deer never will get wise. The more cautious you are about entering and leaving stands, the longer your deer will remain undisturbed and huntable.

CALLS
———

RATTLING ANTLERS

There are those occasions when rattling antlers work like magic, luring in buck after buck, until sometimes there might be three or four in sight at once. At other times, you can rattle until your arms fall off and never see a deer, much less an antler.

Timing is everything. A serious fight usually occurs when two bucks who think they are evenly matched cross paths during the rut. When neither one backs down, war commences. There isn't much point in trying to simulate the sounds of such a battle before does go into heat, it only makes the deer suspicious. The time to rattle is when real bucks are fighting over real does during the rut. The week or ten days immediately before the peak of the rut have historically been the most productive time to rattle.

Chances are this buck won't respond to rattling.

The buck to doe ratio plays a role, too. If the timing is right and there are two or three does per buck, chances are you'll get a response when you rattle. But if every buck has ten or fifteen does to choose from, the likelihood is much lower that he'll race to the sound of a fight. Deer won't respond either if everyone hunting on a property half-heartedly rattles all season long, rattles from treestands, rattles from vehicles, and maybe rattles when they sleep. Deer aren't that dumb.

When the timing is right, rattling works any time of day. Some hunters like to rattle all day long. Some sit on a stand morning and evening and rattle in the middle of the day when deer are normally the most inactive. During the height of the rut, the only time to be rattling anyway, I prefer rattling mornings and afternoons and sitting on a funnel stand between two bedding areas from about nine A.M. until two or three P.M. If pressed, my preference is for late afternoon and evening rattling on a crisp day, when the bucks are rested up and full of vinegar.

The best place to rattle is in fairly thick woods, preferably around the fringes of a bedding area. Since bucks will know within a few feet where the rattling is coming from and usually try to circle downwind, bowhunters have the best chance for a shot by sneaking in from downwind and rattling as a team: one rattler and one or two shooters. To intercept a circling buck, the rattler should be in the center and the shooters about fifty yards away on either side of him at right angles to the wind. They should all set up in deep shade and wear their best camo. If hunting as a team, always know exactly where the other hunters are situated and be certain not to launch an arrow in their direction if a deer passes between you. A broadhead is every bit as deadly as a bullet and can't be recalled once released.

When the hunters are in place and ready for possible instant action, the rattler should clash the antlers together, then grind them against each other for a few seconds. Pull them apart and paw the ground with one and thrash some nearby brush with the other. Grate the antlers together again. Kick a log or roll some rocks with one foot. Beat the base of one antler against the ground a couple of times. If you've ever witnessed a

It's impossible to make too much noise when simulating a take-no-prisoners fight between two mature bucks.

full-blown battle between two evenly matched mature bucks, I don't have to tell you about the train-wreck atmosphere, with crashing antlers, pounding hooves, breaking brush, and the wheezing and gasping of the combatants. You already know that it's hard to make too much noise, at least initially. After twenty or thirty seconds of this, stop and wait a minute or two. Grind the antlers together again, without the initial clash, then paw the ground with one antler. Wait a couple of minutes then just tickle the tips of the antlers together. Wait another five minutes then repeat the entire sequence. I'll usually go through the series two or three times, over a period of twenty minutes or so. Wait silently for at least another fifteen minutes before moving or making a sound. If no deer have responded, it's time to move and try again.

Just as those who bugle for elk during the rut know that real live bulls make every sound imaginable when they're bugling, from a crystal-clear whistle to a strangled groan, buck fights come in every shape and size. It's difficult to rattle incorrectly if the timing is right and you're in the right place, but there are a couple of mistakes to avoid. In a real buck fight, the antlers don't repeatedly crash together like cymbals, but grind and

Does rattling work?

Steve Dollar knows rattling works. He rattled in and shot this tremendous Texas buck at eight paces.

grate as the deer shove and twist while trying to throw each other off balance. And contrary to what has been written in some outdoor magazines, don't use a grunt tube in the midst of rattling. Bucks wheeze and groan and slobber and gasp when fighting, but never once utter a mating grunt. If you wish, a series of grunts can be used after the entire rattling sequence.

You never know how deer will react to rattling. Occasionally, a big dominant buck charges right in, breathing fire, intent upon whipping both combatants and taking any does for himself. More often, he'll move in quickly but cautiously and circle downwind. Sometimes, he'll hang up, refusing to come any closer. A couple of soft grunts often moves him within arrow range. Then again the same deer might approach like a ghost, never giving a hint of his presence until you finally give up and start to leave, and he explodes out of the brush twenty yards away. Sometimes nothing at all happens when you rattle. You might rattle most of the day and get zero response. But if you know your timing is right persevere, for few experiences short of bungie jumping offer the adrenaline surge of rattling in a big buck to mere feet, where he stands with antlers gleaming, eyes blazing, and steam surging from his nostrils. Just make sure your companions know CPR before using rattling antlers in good deer country.

GRUNT TUBES

Like rattling antlers, grunt tubes work only during the rut and grunting at any other time simply alerts the deer that something is amiss. A grunt tube simulates the sound a buck makes when following a doe in heat, very much like a short, soft belch. The buck will often travel at a stiff-legged trot, nose to the doe's trail like a bloodhound, uttering a grunt every few steps.

It is all but impossible to grunt a buck away from a doe, the grunt usually just prompts him to herd his doe away from the sound as quickly as possible. For this reason, I don't like to blindly "prospect" grunt from a stand at regular intervals as some recommend. If an unseen buck with a doe are headed straight for your stand, a grunt simply serves to warn the buck away from what he perceives as competition.

Instead, I use a grunt tube when a lone buck is passing out of range and will not otherwise offer a shot. The grunt tube should be blown very softly when within sight of a buck, just enough to make a sound, though at times you might have to grunt loudly initially to get his attention. In Montana a couple of years ago, I grunted at a nice buck feeding across a river but he ignored me. I realize now he couldn't hear me, but I was ready to climb down from the tree anyway and so blew the tube like a bugle just to pester him. You can understand why I was more than a little surprised when he threw up his head, leaped into the water, and started swimming. He trotted up the bank on my side, streaming water like a dog, and a couple more very soft grunts from the tube gave me a perfect broadside shot at fifteen yards.

Near a bedding area or buck sanctuary during the rut, I will, at times, blindly use a grunt tube. When moving and rattling antlers, at about every third location I'll grunt instead of using the antlers. A series of three or four fairly loud grunts, spaced a few seconds apart and repeated every couple of minutes, sometimes yield more results than the rattling.

In my experience, a grunt tube works best on mature bucks, who are prone to charge up fully prepared to whip the intruder and take his doe. Small and medium-sized bucks are much more circumspect, for the last time they heard the sound they likely got thumped by one of the big guys. A buck who doesn't have his mind on rutting usually ignores the grunt after an

This lone buck, seeking out a doe in heat, is a prime candidate to react to a grunt call.

initial glance. The bucks who respond best are usually the ones who are actively checking does, or traveling about looking for does in heat.

FAWN BLEAT

Over the years, I have used a call which mimics a fawn bleat to kill several does, but found that bucks simply ignored them. Recently, however, I've discovered that at times they work better than a grunt tube when it comes to calling bucks within range. Actually, as much as I would like to take credit for this, my youngest son, Reed, who was ten at the time, first discovered this trick. He tried grunting at a nice buck who was herding a doe, but the buck, naturally, wanted no part of it. As they were leaving, Reed stuck his grunt tube back in a shirt pocket and noticed a fawn bleater. Not knowing any better, he pulled it out

If presented with this scenario during the rut, don't grunt at the buck, but bleat at the doe.

and blew it at the buck. The *doe* stopped in her tracks, then trotted straight to my son's tree. The buck, of course, followed right behind. Reed got a ten yard shot, which, I'm sad to relate, was a miss.

But when he told me this story I was intrigued. Since then, when seeing a mature buck with a doe and knowing how futile a grunt tube would be, I've several times used a fawn bleat *to call the doe.* The buck follows every time. A fawn bleater has given me a couple of dunk shots in otherwise hopeless situations, and now I never leave camp without one during the rut.

STALKING

A ny experienced bowhunter knows how difficult it is to sneak up on a whitetail, though "almost impossible" might better describe the chances on a mature buck. A friend of mine is a wildlife photographer of vast experience who routinely gets within twenty or thirty yards of large whitetails. Though he almost exclusively photographs free-ranging deer, he once learned of a penned buck with an unusual rack he decided to photograph. The deer was confined in a ten acre pen of fairly heavy woods. My friend spent three full days attempting to photograph that buck, and ruefully admits that during the entire period he actually watched the deer for a total of less than five minutes. Though he finally came away with the pictures he wanted, he also came away with enormous respect for the big buck's consummate elusiveness.

Though no one should underestimate the difficulty of approaching deer while on foot, "almost impossible" is not the same as "totally out of the question." Every year really big bucks are taken by stalking bowhunters. One factor which greatly effects the feasibility of stalking with a bow is the hunting pressure on the deer. A few years ago I hunted in Montana. The big ranch was very lightly hunted, and no one *ever* hunted in the thick timber where we spent all of our time. I was amazed at how closely you could approach those deer, and a couple of times had nice bucks stand up from their beds and stare at me for a moment at thirty or forty yards. I could have killed several does at under twenty yards.

Under such circumstances, assuming light hunting pressure, it is possible to stalk a deer on foot to within arrow range. The first key to success is seeing the deer before the deer sees you. This is far easier (though easier is a relative term) when the deer are moving rather than bedded. Early mornings, late evenings, and anytime during the rut is the time to stalk travel

The chances of sneaking up on this bedded buck are virtually zero...

...but a stealthy bowhunter does have an outside chance of getting a shot at a buck such as this who is on the move.

I climbed down from a treestand and began a long stalk when I saw this Pope and Young buck walking a quarter mile away. Finally, I was positioned along the deer's line of travel and made the broadside shot ten seconds later when he stepped into the open.

or bedding areas, when the deer are on the move. This type of stalking is not a matter of walking right up to a stationary or bedded deer, but seeing him moving and positioning yourself undetected ahead of him then letting him come to you. I've had some success during the rut stalking in thick woods and setting up on moving deer. One of the best bucks I've taken this way prompted me to climb down from a treestand one morning and stalk across several hundred yards of low-growing cedars. After thirty minutes of nerve-racking "tag" in the cover, he made the mistake of offering me a broadside shot.

A consistently successful stalker psyches himself out to a Zen-level state of concentration and focus, until he wears the woods like an overcoat. It might take a couple of hours to travel a hundred yards in thick cover. A pair of binoculars is essential for this type of hunting, and you should look through them five times more than you actually move. Sit down frequently or stand still for ten or fifteen minutes. If you move slowly enough, you're not moving at all as far as the deer are concerned, which allows you to penetrate places unnoticed where the deer feel secure enough to wander about freely. Once a buck is spotted, you may have to make a quick lateral dash to cut him off. A chilly, cloudy day after a front moves through during the rut, ideally with the ground and leaves damp, is the best time for stalking. Wool clothing belongs in such weather for its warmth and silence.

In thick woods bedded deer, especially the big guys, tend to

A drizzling rain during the rut is one of the primary times bucks like this are moving and vulnerable to stalking.

sidestep a single human and circle downwind of him. Once, from a distance, I watched a nice buck evade a hunter headed into the wind through the thick tangle of a river bend. The hunter jumped several bedded doe and yearlings which he pushed out ahead of him. They all splashed across a shallow ford of the river and passed ten yards from where I waited. The buck came out on the trail behind the does and stood in the screen of brush on the riverbank. You could almost hear him thinking as he used his ears to exactly pinpoint the unseen hunter behind. The mature deer glanced across the river where the does had disappeared and where I sat in invisible ambush. He finally decided, "Nope. Not today," then ducked his head and melted back into the brush of the river bend. In three minutes the hunter appeared right where the buck had vanished, never aware that a trophy deer had just outmaneuvered him at a range under thirty yards. On another occasion, in a high wind which covered movement and sound, I stalked through a bedding area of thick mesquites and tall grass. Because of the conditions, I closed to within ten yards of at least a dozen bedded deer that day. Trouble was, they were invisible until they flushed at a run. Shooting at one would have been like shooting at flying quail.

If such bedded deer detect you when you're stalking, as they almost always will, one hunter doesn't stand a chance of getting a shot. For those big bucks who can easily skirt one mere human on foot and has done so many times in the past, stalking can actually work better with two hunters, though intuition might at first tell you otherwise. While moving at the same pace into the wind, one man trails about fifty to a hundred yards behind the other, keeping just barely within sight of the leader. When deer detect the first hunter, they often sidestep and circle around unseen to the downwind side, where they can keep track of the human and his progress. If the spacing is right, these deer can walk right into the lap of the second hunter. In thick brush, the trailer should stay alert for moving deer at very close ranges. He should also be prepared to move quickly to one side to cut off a circling buck.

One useful refinement which can often buy some time is to use a diaphragm or other call to give an occasional turkey cluck as you move through the woods (this should only be attempted on private property where you know who is hunting—on public ground the chances of being accidentally shot by some rifle-armed yahoo are far too great). Deer are well aware of a wild turkey's remarkable alertness and eyesight and tend to relax when undisturbed turkeys are around.

Perfect camouflage, patience, and industrial-strength luck can add up to stalking success. It won't happen every day, or even every season, but it *can* happen. Certainly there is no purer way to kill a deer, and please take my word for it that one nice buck taken this way will overshadow hunting success with just about any other method.

DRIVES

The problem with a standard deer drive is that it is very difficult to *force* a mature buck to move. He has the nerves of a sword swallower when he thinks he's being driven. Just one example. A large ranch I'm familiar with was doing a deer survey by helicopter late this past summer. One of the nice bucks they found, in the 160" class, was in a thin patch of woods smaller than an acre. Though they spent almost ten minutes trying to chase him from his hideout for a photograph, repeatedly buzzing him with the helicopter at ranges of only a few feet, he never panicked and flatly refused to be driven away from his cover.

The term "drive" is a misnomer, really, as it applies to bowhunters, for a properly executed one bears no resemblance to the tiger drives that rifle hunters frequently conduct. The real trick to it is that the deer must never realize they're being driven, but believe they are sneaking away and escaping. It should be more of a gentle nudge than a drive.

A buck who realizes he's being driven will as often as not sneak away unnoticed or lie down and hide.

Unless the area will not be hunted again for several weeks, drives shouldn't be conducted early in the season, for they serve to unnecessarily force the deer into nocturnal activity and the thickest cover. If you have numerous places to hunt, however, early drives can compel deer to move when the weather is too hot, which is often the case down South during archery season. Late in the fall, after the deer are already on alert, drives are an excellent tactic for making them move in the daytime. Then is the time to drive the bedding areas which you've carefully kept sacrosanct all season long.

Drives are very specialized as they work best when the deer are confined to a long narrow strip of brush. In general cover, the deer can scatter in any direction, and there's no predicting where they'll go. Thick timber along a riverbottom, with water on one side and open grassland on the other is tailor-made for drives. So are long woodlots bordered by cropfields. Here in Texas, the uplands are often cleared of brush and the creeks and drainages left in heavy cover, an ideal set-up for drives. Check your aerial photo for any area which fits this description, then plan your drives just before season's end.

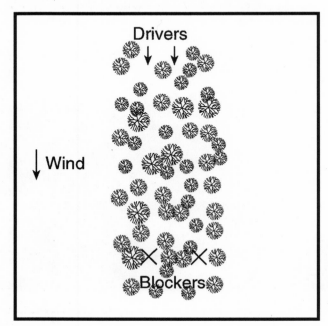

The standard deer drive with the wind. The biggest bucks are difficult to move with this scenario.

A standard drive consists of blockers, who wait on the deer's escape routes, and the drivers, whose movement through the cover influences the deer into motion away from them. Drives have a couple of basic ground rules which are closely related. The drivers should move slowly, at no more than an easy walk, so the deer will be less inclined to resort to running flight through the timber or breaking out of the cover into the open. And no matter what the circumstances, blockers should not attempt running shots, as they usually lead to bad hits and wounded game.

Wind can be an important factor on a drive. Most try to set up where the drivers start on the upwind side of the cover and move with the wind. The man-scent drifting to the deer (which can be enhanced with predator scent or even cigarette smoke) helps move them out far in advance of the drivers, so far, in fact, that the drivers may not ever see a deer though they push a dozen or more out ahead of them. The deer will be forced to move downwind and cannot detect the waiting blockers. Exactly this scenario has worked well for me in the past but I've also found a problem with it. The big mature bucks, who have seen it all, are very reluctant to move away from a man-made

A better tactic for a drive if mature bucks are the aim. The bucks are more likely to move ahead of the drivers, as planned, instead of hiding or breaking across the openings bordering the strip of woods. Note how the blockers are staggered, so the cross-wind doesn't blow one hunter's scent directly toward the other.

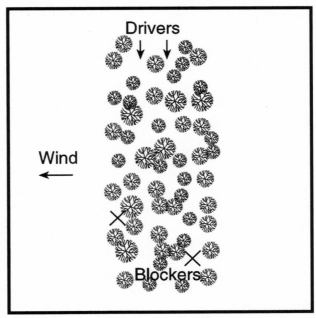

disturbance with the wind at their backs. When the wind favors a predator waiting in ambush, the big guys are just as likely to lie down and hide, letting the drivers walk right past them, or daringly break back past the drivers into the wind, or escape across the open ground surrounding the woods. I've repeatedly seen really big bucks do these things more often than I've seen them travel with the wind past the blockers. They got big by rarely making mistakes.

If you're after mature bucks, the answer lies in conducting drives only in a crosswind situation. You have to let him *think* he has every advantage while he's avoiding the humans. If he has a crosswind or an angling headwind, he'll be much more likely to travel as predicted and move past the blockers. Cover scent is called for here and, in addition, at least one blocker should be near the downwind edge of the stretch of timber, where most big deer will tend to pass.

How much distance should the drive cover? While even short drives of a couple hundred yards often yield results, if terrain conditions are favorable up to half a mile can be driven. Longer drives are theoretically possible but deer are difficult to move in a straight line for very far, they start circling and trying to evade the drivers or break out of the timber.

If a road crosses the woods, or evergreens change to hardwoods, or the cover thins out, the blockers should set up fifty to a hundred yards back into the woods from these places. Deer moving in front of drivers will generally stop back in the thicker woods before crossing the more open area. Here they'll wait, milling about and watching behind them to see if the danger is still coming. Blockers will usually have a chance to look over potential bucks and have a stationary shot. Rather than set up in front of a tree or bush as most hunters are inclined to do, he should stand or kneel *behind* the cover to help hide the movement of drawing his bow. Once the deer are sure the drivers are getting close they'll grow more and more nervous and finally break out at a run across the opening. Anyone set up right on the road or other open area will have nothing but shooting gallery running shots, which should be studiously avoided.

An alternative is to sit a treestand in a potential drive area from before daylight as usual, then have companions stage a

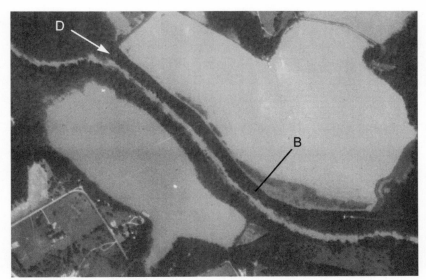

Set-up for drives through narrow stretches of woods. Blockers (B) and drivers (D).

Blockers (B) and drivers (D) are standard. A big buck might well try to slip out the escape route (E), so one blocker should be positioned here.

drive past it about nine o'clock. This is my favorite method for conducting drives, especially larger ones with several treestand sitters and drivers, for then you have the entire day to follow up hits on two or more deer as sometimes results from a well-planned and executed hunt of this type. For those bowhunters who have never tried a drive, it's difficult to describe the adrenaline overload of watching thirty deer, half of them bucks, pass by at rock-throwing distance. The first time it happens, you're almost guaranteed to wet your pants, and I've often gathered up ashen-faced blockers after such a drive who were shaking their heads and mumbling.

Another option is a one man drive, conducted early in the afternoon. Starting at a feeding area such as an agricultural field, the hunter walks a long strip of woods through a bedding area and beyond, flushing deer away from him as he goes. He then stops and sets up on the ground or in a pre-positioned treestand on the downwind portion of the timber. Here he waits until dark. The deer usually will stop soon after the hunter stops, and either mill about or eventually bed down again. Then, as evening approaches, they will begin to filter back towards the feeding area, keeping to the downwind side of the cover. Deer in most areas, and especially in farming country, are used to some human disturbance and normally don't over-react. Once the disturbance ends, they cautiously go back to their routine, moving with a sort of hydraulic pressure into the deer vacuum created by the drive. A couple of additional moves on the hunter's part can improve this technique. Make the disturbance one the deer expect. Have a hunting partner start a chainsaw, and rev it occasionally, while staying with you while you walk to your stand site. Then he leaves the woods, with the saw still running, while you set up. If there is another entrance to the food source you have pushed the deer away from, it would pay your partner to put away his chainsaw and go sit there for the evening.

Remember, such drives are last-ditch efforts to move the deer after they've become unhuntable by "normal" means. It's surprising how often such a crazy tactic as driving deer with a chainsaw actually works, so don't be afraid to try something just as outrageous late in the season.

The author with a heavy-horned four-by-four, shot from the ground at under five paces on a Montana deer drive.

Using others to conduct what I call an inadvertent drive can work anytime during the season. A classic example is the wise hunter who has scouted a public hunting area and knows the locations of funnels on escape routes to the heaviest timber or adjoining private land. Then, the day before the public hunting begins, he slips far back into the area with a light pack, spends the night, and before daylight moves into his pre-determined position. He waits there all day, secure in the knowledge that the other hunters with less initiative and knowledge of deer habits will fan out from their parking areas and conduct a massive drive towards his escape route. I know a man who kills a deer with a bow almost every year using precisely this method, and this in an area which sees an archery success rate during the week-long season of well under five percent.

You should keep your eyes and ears open for other opportunities for inadvertent drives. A farmer where you hunt is harvesting a field of corn? You can bet that he'll push deer out of the tall cover of the corn as he does so, and maybe some big bucks among them. Determine how the harvest will proceed and set up on trails leading to cover on the opposite side of the field. Keep in mind that deer are more likely to use the exit in a cross wind than in a tail wind. Always be alert for such a situation which might develop; a rancher using horses to gather cattle from a pasture, a landowner cutting firewood in a woodlot, the opening of duck or quail season with its birdhunters and dogs.

One sunrise a few seasons back, I was startled to hear a bulldozer crank its engine four or five hundred yards from my treestand. My disgust soon turned to predatory concentration when I noticed a fine ten-point buck headed my way. He wasn't really frightened, only moving at a steady trot, but was clearly unwilling to share his patch of woods with a D7 Caterpillar. He was too preoccupied to notice anyone drawing a bow and I'm delighted to report that he did not survive our encounter. In all fairness, that unwitting dozer operator deserves a big assist for the kill.

ANY unusual disturbance can potentially be used to great advantage by the alert bowhunter.

HUNTING THE BIG GUYS

Before contemplating hunting one of the big guys, it might be beneficial to first consider what constitutes a trophy to a traditional bowhunter. To the average rifle hunter, a trophy is defined as a buck with large antlers, usually measured against the standards of the Boone and Crockett system. Whitetail rifle hunters compare their results to the biggest bucks taken anywhere in the country, often 190 net inches or sometimes even more. The average compound bowhunter, too, sees archers taking 170 and 180 inch deer every month in the magazines and compares his results to theirs.

The trophy is in the eye of the beholder.

Just as a mountain climber scorns a helicopter ride to the top of the peak, so recurve and longbow shooters have chosen a different route. Their motivation is the contest of the archer against himself and the individual deer rather than against some faceless stranger hunting the prime areas of North America. Competition is the last reason we take our longbows to the woods.

Which is not to say that traditional archers don't hunt hard, quite the contrary, for most work harder for a chance at a trophy than any six rifle hunters. Many traditional archers have come to think of a trophy buck in one of three ways. He can be any mature (read experienced and crafty) buck, four and a half years or older, no matter what his antler size. Or a trophy can be any buck which qualifies for the minimum Pope and Young records of 125 net inches. Or a trophy can be any buck with antlers large enough to represent the top end of what a particular area has to offer, which may range from 115 inches up to 180 inches depending upon the location. In order to more accurately evaluate bucks in the field, deer-judging videos such as the excellent tape by John Wooters and Larry Weishuhn should be watched several times before the season begins.

In other cases, however, the *way* a deer is taken has as much bearing on its "trophy" status as the size of the antlers. That forkhorn buck stalked on the ground and shot with a longbow in the public hunting area of Pennsylvania is just as much a trophy as a 156 inch ten-point another hunter picked from dozens of big bucks on a prime South Texas ranch. I've taken numerous "small" bucks from the ground which represent, to my mind, more of a trophy and more accomplishment than other "large" bucks taken from treestands. You have to decide what constitutes a trophy based upon where and how you hunt.

However you define the term, hunting a trophy buck with a bow is many times more difficult than hunting just any generic deer, whether you're after one specific mature buck or simply holding out for a rack of a particular size. I'm convinced that with each passing year of their lives, male deer become twice as hard to hunt as they were the year before. Which means that— not even considering their relative scarcity—a mature buck will be about ten times more difficult than a young one.

In a very heavily hunted area of Tennessee, Brad Smith scouted and found where the deer were eating acorns. He used one of his handmade black locust selfbows to take this forkhorn buck at twelve yards. Is this a trophy? You'd better believe it!

Throughout the hunting season, whether before, during, or after the rut, the hunter of big bucks has to be more subtle and much more precise. You'll have to resign yourself to seeing fewer deer, for your overall hunting strategy has to change when you're concentrating on a trophy. Earlier, the plan was to hunt staging areas near food sources first, then work back toward bedding areas as the season progressed. The very biggest bucks are the last to leave bedding areas in the evening, and the first to return to them in the morning, even with no hunting pressure. So now the strategy is to get as close to the bedding areas as we dare from the very beginning of the season. The hunter concentrating on the big guys constantly examines his maps and plans his travel routes. Stealth and a perfect entry and exit from stands becomes more important than before, for mature bucks which have been alerted that they are being hunted become almost unkillable.

As the rut approaches, the trophy hunter relies more and more on rattling and grunting. Once the rut actually begins, he should stay in the field all day. Continue to rattle and grunt and also use stands in secondary funnels between bedding areas, especially from ten in the morning until three in the afternoon when big bucks often move while searching for does. A surprisingly large percentage of record book whitetails have been taken during the rut between late morning and early afternoon. Normally, I'll rattle early and late and sit in a stand the rest of the day.

Astute whitetail hunters also make it a point to be in the woods immediately before and after big storm fronts. The deer have always seemed especially active just after a storm ends. One November, after three days of sleet, ten degree temperatures, and a thirty mile an hour wind, the sun finally broke free of the clouds early in the afternoon. The deer were hungry after being pinned down by the storm so long and flocked to a wheatfield. I've never seen so many deer, including mature bucks, moving. On a similar note, when the rut is just beginning but the weather has been warm, a cold front often sets off a flurry of rutting activity. Woods which seemed quiet suddenly come alive with deer. There's no better time to be afield with a bow.

If your mission in life is to take a trophy buck and you don't mind the possibility of blowing out a bedding area by hunting within it, unobtrusive treestands should be placed in these areas well before the season starts. During the rut, deer will be

During the rut, deer move all day in the cover of bedding areas.

moving all day within the safety of the thick cover. Occasional rattling from a stand often pays off in this situation. Don't forget the grunt call if you see a lone buck passing out of range and the fawn bleat if you see a buck with a doe. Enter the stand before daylight and plan to tough it out all day—take a snack, water bottle, and urine bottle. As golfer Byron Nelson once noted, "golf is a game of luck. The harder I work, the luckier I get". So should the bowhunter intent on a trophy buck increase his luck by working hardest during the rut.

At the peak of the rut, spot and stalk methods can pay off for whitetails, for many times a buck will herd a doe in heat out into more open areas. The nimble hunter can sometimes spot such a pair from a distance and place the sneak on them while their attention is diverted. Several times during the rut we have seen a buck and a doe out in the open while driving a ranch road and quietly dropped off a hunter without stopping. The deer nonchalantly watch the vehicle disappear and remain unaware of the nearby hunter.

Stalking during the rut often yields results for the deer move all day and moving deer, even mature bucks, are vulnerable to

The rut is about the only time a buck like this lets down his guard.

Paul Anselmo and a buck which was a little too intent upon chasing a doe.

a careful stalker. A heavy rain tends to dampen deer activity but a light drizzle is ideal for moving silently through the woods during the rut. While your hunting buddies are back at camp taking a nap or cursing the weather, you should always be afield under such conditions. Good quality wool clothing will both keep you dry and silence your movements. Many times I've eased slowly into the wind during a light rain and spent the day playing tag with deer in the thick cover of a bedding area. I've had pretty fair success bowhunting this way and for my money few methods are more enjoyable or exciting.

As soon as the rut winds down, surviving larger bucks usually vanish into a sanctuary, never to be seen by hunters again. Think of this from the deer's point of view. Most humans are noisy in the woods, smell bad, hunt from or near a vehicle, and are harmless at night. It's a simple matter to avoid them, for they are only dangerous in the open in the daytime.

Hunting a reclusive buck after the rut is where post-season scouting the year before really pays off. A hunter who has found a big buck's sanctuary with its tell-tale large rubs knows where to go when average hunters have shrugged their shoulders and given up for the year. To find a sanctuary, a hunter familiar with a property should ask, "Where do the hunters on this place never go? Where would I go if someone were hunting me?" The topo map and aerial photo will be invaluable in helping to answer these questions. Most sanctuaries are relatively small, a half acre up to forty acres or so. The cover is invariably thick and the location unlikely, which is why the bucks hiding there are seldom disturbed.

A big ranch I've hunted for several years in Montana is joined by fifty acres of thick woods whose owner allows no hunting. Guess where the big bucks go when they feel hunting pressure? A couple of treestands just inside the big ranch's property line have proven deadly for Pope and Young deer.

While recently scouting during the off-season, I found a sanctuary on a Central Texas property by accident, while walking the perimeter fence looking for crossings. After a large rub caught my eye, nearby I discovered more big rubs and the isolated one acre patch of impenetrable cedars on a rocky hillside a mature buck used as a hideout. The sanctuary was so

As a rule, only the biggest bucks rub the larger trees.

The sure sign of a mature buck. Rubs on large trees adjacent to a thick, secluded sanctuary. Tree in foreground is freshly rubbed, while second tree has healed rubs from the year before, both almost certainly used by the same buck.

well chosen it had likely been years since any human had ventured into it. Though I have yet to see him, this fall I plan to get much better acquainted with the buck living there.

In the Yellowstone River in Montana lies a two acre island covered with logs, cottonwood saplings, and rose thickets. Once hunting season opens, the landowner assured me that the biggest bucks swim out to the island and swim back every evening after dark to the alfalfa fields along the riverbottom. Though I never got a chance to try it, I would love to float down to the island in a boat an hour before dawn and be waiting when the bucks returned to their hideout just at daylight. A friend from the northeast uses an equally unlikely tactic to take

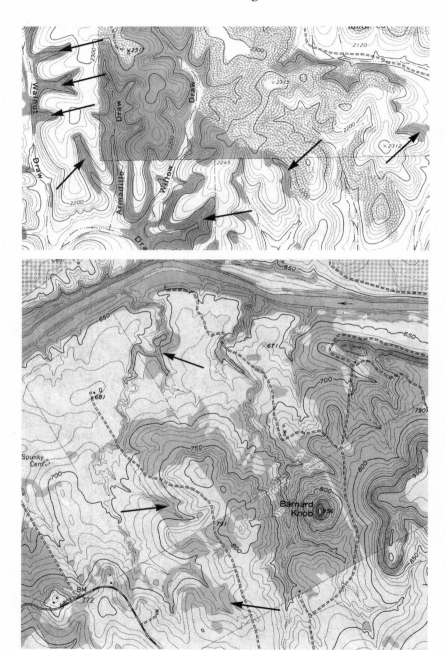

Look for sanctuaries in isolated pockets of heavy cover, especially those on small drainages.

a mature buck almost every season. He places a treestand in the heavily timbered islands created in the *medians of an interstate highway!* The big bucks know perfectly well where they won't be bothered and gravitate to these improbable sanctuaries once the shooting starts.

When searching for such sanctuaries, remember to ask, "Where do the hunters never go?" Scour your maps for isolated pockets of heavy woods, or areas of thick evergreens among more open hardwoods, or islands in a swamp, or any other area which is inaccessible to the average hunter. Here in Texas, I've seen mature bucks bedded in the middle of vast prickly pear cactus flats, which yields them almost invincible to a stalk. Sometimes, big deer choose unbelievably small spots for their hideouts, like a sumac thicket on an open hillside. I once found

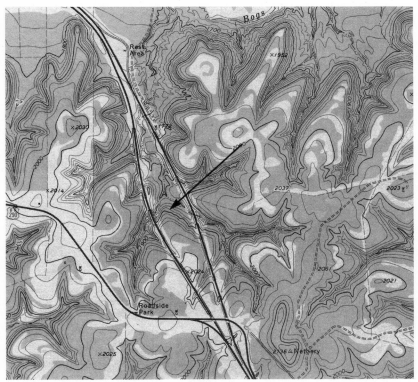

With surrounding hunting pressure, this "island" sanctuary created by an interstate highway will be a magnet for mature bucks.

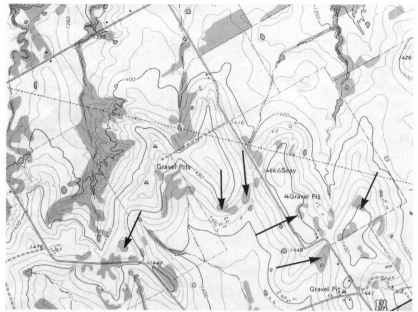

Don't overlook small patches of cover when searching for sanctuaries.

This dominant buck has just left his sanctuary late in the afternoon and has been rubbing wrist-thick saplings.

a sanctuary in a brush-choked ditch only ten yards wide between two large alfalfa fields, a place where you'd never expect to find a deer, which, naturally, was why he chose the spot.

Wherever they're located, the sure sign of a sanctuary is a concentration of three or four (or more) large rubs on trees greater than three inches in diameter. After a big buck has rested all day he's full of vinegar when he gets up in the evenings and can't resist aggressively rubbing on some nearby trees. Scrapes are often found in conjunction with the rubs, which makes the location all the better. You might check a dozen likely places for sanctuaries for every one you find, but the certain evidence of paydirt will be the big rubs. Mark such places on your map, then keep them inviolate by never going near them until conditions are perfect.

How to hunt a sanctuary?

Ideally, a sanctuary is first discovered after hunting season closes, when you can scout without fear of contaminating an area with your scent or flushing the buck living there. Scout the area thoroughly to discover how the deer enters and leaves the hideout. He'll probably have several trails into and out of his sanctuary, for use under different wind conditions. If you're lucky, you can find tracks showing which trails are entrances and which are exits; sometimes they are one and the same. Once again, the maps will be of great assistance as they reveal how he's using the terrain and most likely where he's going.

Carefully consider prevailing wind direction when examining his trails to and from the location. Heavily hunted big bucks play the wind like a fiddle during the daytime, when their primary predator, man, is active (after dark, however, when men are harmless, deer don't hesitate to travel with the wind. In moderate or lightly hunted areas they also regularly move with the wind at their backs). But remember that a mature buck facing hunting pressure hesitates to use a trail during daylight unless he thinks the wind is in his favor, so his trails should now begin to make sense. When the time comes, at the very least you'll have to play a crosswind situation for he won't appear if the wind is to his disadvantage. Take this into consideration when considering possible treestand locations or

After the rut ends, wise bucks generally move in the daytime only with the wind in their favor.

This buck is using a tiny patch of cattails and willows for a sanctuary, an area hunters have overlooked.

ground blinds. In this situation, treestands should be hung no less than a month before the season and preferably three or four months.

A mature buck will be almost unapproachable by day when he's bedded in this type location, but he still leaves to drink and eat each and every night. In fact, this is his main concern after the rut as he tries to add a reserve of fat for the winter. The best time to try for such a deer is to slip into the predetermined stand well before daylight, always considering wind direction, of course. Don't even *think* about hunting if the wind is the least bit fickle, for you have no room for error; let him wind you one time and he'll likely change sanctuaries for weeks, if not permanently. The strategy of this set-up is to get a shot just at dawn as the buck returns from his night's ramblings.

An evening ambush is trickier, for he'll be home and your approach to the stand will have to be flawless. But if you're certain you can slip in undetected, set up right on the rubs. Most evenings he'll spend some time rubbing before leaving for his nightly rounds. If he doesn't show by dark, leave just as quietly as you entered, for he may well be still bedded down nearby and remain unaware of your presence. This past season, I entered just such a treestand late one afternoon after a careful stalk of an hour. The plan worked to perfection and put me in close proximity to an excellent buck, only it worked TOO well, since instead of using the rubs ten yards away he strolled up to the base of my tree. This put his head eight feet from the bottom of my stand where he stood like a statue for a couple of minutes, letting me admire his eyelashes and flaring nostrils and ten heavy points. Finally, he sniffed a tree step at eye level next to him and instantly bolted. Though I never drew the bow I considered such a close encounter a victory nonetheless. It only took twenty minutes for the shakes to subside enough so I could climb down from that stand.

In some of the larger sanctuaries of five acres or more, dominant bucks during the rut can be huntable. It's tricky, but sometimes this is the only look you'll ever get at a really reclusive, nocturnal buck. Such a deer leaves his sanctuary at night, finds a doe in or near heat, and herds her back to his hideout. After twenty-four to forty-eight hours, when the doe has been

During the rut, bucks often move about within one of their sanctuaries with a doe in heat.

bred and gone out of heat, the buck will leave in the darkness to find another doe. You can't ambush him entering or leaving but if you can slip undetected into a prepositioned stand in a downwind portion of his sanctuary, he may offer a shot in the thick cover as he moves about with his doe during the daylight hours. Such hunting can be monumentally boring, for chances are you won't see a deer. But if you *do* see one, it could be the one that we're all after, the one most hunters never suspect exists on their property. Sometimes a partner can slowly drive or walk by the upwind side of the sanctuary when you're in position and send the deer moving to the downwind side.

With careful pre-season scouting of a large enough area, a hunter can usually find eight or ten sanctuaries, more than enough to keep him entertained after the rut. He can try a different place each day, depending upon wind, and stands a decent chance of taking a big mature buck at a time other hunters find impossible.

If all else fails and it's late in the season, you can try a

A buck will know every nook and cranny of his sanctuary, as well as every conceivable escape route should he detect trouble.

full-fledged drive on a sanctuary if it has been well-scouted and the exits discovered. One or two hunters posted on the escape trails may get a shot as he leaves. Never forget that a buck is very difficult to predict if he realizes he's being driven; he'll either hide like a rabbit or explode out in whichever direction he happens to be facing. But usually he'll sneak away if he thinks he's escaping. The driver can try the chainsaw ploy, mentioned earlier. Or maybe walk in from well upwind carrying a rag soaked in Liquid Smoke or dog urine. Or two drivers can stroll to within a hundred yards of the upwind side of the sanctuary and hold a loud prolonged conversation on the relative merits of recurves vs. longbows before starting the drive.

Don't be afraid to try something just this outrageous late in the season. The big guys have you figured out by now because they pattern hunters a lot faster than hunters pattern them. If you haven't yet connected, redouble your efforts instead of getting discouraged and sloppy for that only makes it easier for the deer. Be assured that if your property is moderately hunted, the mature bucks are still there somewhere, even though they might seem to have been vaporized. Along with your maps, advanced scouting, and observations in the field, use your reasoning powers to try to ascertain how a big guy has been evading you and where he's hiding. Then proceed to outsmart him and formulate a plan, and don't worry if it's unorthodox. Try carrying a transistor radio if you're a driver on a deer drive. Hunt two hundred yards from camp. Climb down from a treestand and sprint a quarter mile to cut off a distant buck. Look on your maps and select the most inaccessible place to hunt, somewhere that you've never been. Such tactics don't always work, of course, but throwing a wise old buck a curve may be the only way to get a chance at him late in the season and these off-the-wall moves which a deer has never encountered work often enough to be worthwhile.

If the biggest deer on a property is a two and a half year old eight-point, killing a Pope and Young buck is, of course, out of the question. You can't kill what isn't there. Even if one or two trophy bucks are present, you might well never see them or even suspect their presence. But if twenty-five such deer are in your hunting area, you stand an excellent chance of not only seeing one, but taking him with a bow. We can have a profound effect upon herd composition and greatly increase the number of trophies present by the animals we choose to kill—our management of a place.

Management begins with the three things which determine the size of a buck's antlers: genetics, nutrition, and age.

Almost every deer herd contains the genetics for large antlers. Check the record books and photos and you'll find tremendous bucks from such seemingly unlikely places as Delaware, Maine, Kentucky, Kansas, and New Hampshire. Since genetics is the one variable over which hunters have little control, this is good news, indeed.

Genetics helped produce these wonderful antlers.

Nutrition is a factor over which hunters can exercise tremendous influence, for by cropping enough does so that the remaining herd has abundant forage, antler size can be improved. By keeping deer numbers below the carrying capacity of a place, not only does each deer have more to eat, but the plant composition improves, as well. When a herd is overpopulated the hungry deer kill off the most palatable, nutritious plants first before switching to less desirable forage. Keeping deer numbers well below carrying capacity also offers some cushion against die-offs when a particularly hard winter or dry summer stresses the herd. Cropping does to manage deer numbers serves to improve the buck to doe ratio as well, which makes for more competition and movement during the rut and greatly improves tactics such as rattling or grunting. State wildlife biologists can advise you on deer densities and recommended doe harvests.

Such a scene usually means very limited trophy prospects.

The third factor which effects antler size is the age of the buck. Until a buck reaches maturity his body expends most of its energy building bone, muscle, and tissue, with little left over for antler growth. After his body has reached its full size at about four and half years of age, then it has far more resources available for manufacturing antlers. Though it may at first

A 3 ½ year old buck, with nice antlers.

The same buck at 6 1/2 years old, with tremendous antlers.

147

sound ridiculous, the way to have more trophy bucks on a given property is to shoot only trophy bucks. By holding out for a trophy, a hunter who passes up the opportunity to kill young bucks allows them to grow to their full potential. Deer judging videos show bucks of many different ages and suggests keys such as body shape and neck size to help the bowhunter evaluate a deer's age in the field. Accurately aging deer prevents the killing of exceptional two and three year old bucks, who at maturity might grow tremendous 160" antlers, or maybe even more. Such a strategy of taking only mature bucks takes discipline, especially for a bowhunter with limited experience, so a reasonable method might be to shoot only bucks larger than those a hunter has killed before. Don't settle for anything less, even at the cost of going home empty-handed. The experience gained and improvement to the deer herd will soon foster success.

Shoot enough does to keep the herd in check and let the young and middle-aged bucks grow up: such management for trophies can have a remarkable impact on the size of the bucks. Only one person, of course, can have little impact on the deer herd, for if he passes on a buck the chances are the next hunter will shoot him. Cooperative management, for this reason, is all but impossible on public land or any land without parameters for its hunters. This is why the concept of hunting leases and hunting clubs have gained such appeal, in spite of the protests of many western hunters who are outraged by the prospect of having to pay to hunt. A group of hunters with like objectives can control enough land to improve the quality and quantity of the trophies. Ten bowhunters, for example, might lease a three thousand acre tract and vow to shoot only does and mature bucks. The last weekend of the season they may have to use rifles to take enough does to meet their management objectives. After two or three years, they will likely be amazed at the size of the bucks they begin harvesting with their arrows.

We should all work to improve our home areas, for therein lies the real future of hunting and trophy deer, but an additional option is to travel to a vast, well-managed ranch in one of the prime trophy areas of North America. A trip to Alberta or Texas

By taking does,
Ted Crow and
Barry Hardin
have not only
harvested some
excellent
venison, but
have helped the
overall deer
herd and future
trophy
prospects, as
well.

or Montana is not cheap, running upwards of two thousand dollars. But for those who live and breathe whitetails, the chance to see thirty Pope and Young bucks in four days as we did last year during a bowhunting clinic I conducted here in Texas, can become a religious experience difficult to explain in mere monetary terms.

MAKING THE SHOT

At this point, the hard part's done. All the scouting, setting stands, poring over maps, and the cerebral gymnastics required to outsmart a buck are complete. There he stands, twenty yards away, totally unaware of your presence. Sure, the hard part's done. All you have to do now is make the shot while surfing on an adrenaline tidalwave. You might plan all year and hunt all season for this two seconds of truth, so you may as well go ahead and make a perfect killing shot.

Making the shot under these circumstances requires three things; practice, practice, and—you guessed it—practice. But simply standing in front of a target and shooting thousands of arrows won't necessarily insure accuracy in the woods. The thousands of arrows must be shot correctly with an eye toward the ultimate goal of taking a deer.

If you're just beginning or are currently experiencing shooting woes, G. Fred Asbell's *Instinctive Shooting* books are required reading. While explaining many options in form, he details exactly how to accurately shoot a traditional bow. Once you settle on a style which feels comfortable, the key lies in shooting precisely the same way every time. One trick for a beginner is to shoot a very light bow, one of thirty pounds or so, for it can quickly help "groove" your shooting form.

Once your form becomes second nature, switch to your hunting bow. You'll especially appreciate choosing a moderate weight bow of around fifty pounds now, so you can shoot a hundred arrows without growing fatigued. Stop whenever you begin growing tired, for then your shooting form collapses and bad habits such as short drawing or plucking the string rear its ugly head.

While practicing, shoot at a tiny spot on the target, this in preparation for picking and shooting at one spot on a deer. If you shoot at the entire hay bale, you'll hit the hay bale, if you shoot at a paper plate, you'll hit the paper plate, but if you shoot at a dime, it's surprising how often you'll hit the dime. Start off at ten yards or less to reinforce consistent arrow placement. Remember that twenty arrows shot with concentration are far better than two hundred shot haphazardly.

If you hit a rocky stretch, as you very likely will, it often helps to return to the light bow for a few days. This easy-to-pull bow allows you to concentrate on your form and release without strain. With experience, you'll probably pick up keys to watch for when you encounter accuracy problems. Fred Asbell points his left arm toward the target, like pointing a finger. When I begin scattering arrows, concentrating on a small spot on the target and consciously anchoring with my right hand immediately shrinks the groups. Some lock their left elbows or exaggerate the follow through and hold their position until the arrow strikes the target. With enough practice, you'll find a key or two which will quickly eliminate any accuracy problems.

Use whatever form works for you. If you watched ten excellent instinctive shooters, their styles would all be different, sometimes radically so. But the one thing they would have in common is that they shoot the same way with every arrow. And they practice a lot. My style has been adapted strictly to deer hunting—I have my left arm holding the bow pointed directly at the deer as soon as he steps out, then draw the arrow straight back with my right arm. This method causes less movement than swinging the bow up from the waist as the arrow is drawn, a style many excellent shooters employ.

If you plan to wear camo gloves and a face veil while hunting, you should also wear them when practicing. Personally, I can't shoot with a cloth face veil, it changes the feel of anchoring the middle finger of my right hand at the corner of my mouth. Wearing no face camo only makes me more meticulous about stand selection and cover. If you wish to be totally camoed and you find that a face veil affects your shooting, camo face paint is the alternative.

Those who hunt from treestands should practice shooting down from an elevation. Even an excellent shot, if unaccustomed to shooting downward, will invariably hit six to twelve inches high depending upon the angle and range. In field conditions, traditional bowhunters shoot over ten whitetails for every one they shoot under, and failing to practice from an elevation is one of the primary reasons. Practice very close, seven to ten yards, for you'll get more of these shots than you'd think, and they're a lot easier to miss than you'd think, too, especially when shooting down (a hunting buddy, Brad Smith, refers to these as "the dreaded ten yard shot"). Also shoot at long ranges, forty yards, even though you'll never take such a

Practice shooting close, because you'll get more of these ten yard shots than you think.

shot at a game animal. Watching the arrow arc into the target from a distance is not only beautiful but helps you get used to your bow and its capabilities.

Along with shooting at various ranges, practice shooting from odd positions, just like you'll face under real hunting conditions. Practice while kneeling, squatting, sitting on the ground, sitting in a chair, standing on one foot (no, I'm not kidding—stalkers often get caught in between steps by deer), shooting straight down, and facing one way and twisting your body to shoot 180 degrees behind you. You'll experience all of these shots and more if you spend much time in the deer woods and the time to discover that arrows shot from a kneeling position, for example, might tend to fly high and left is not when in the presence of a Pope and Young buck.

Competing with friends is an enjoyable way to practice and adds a realistic element of pressure to each shot. Follow-the-leader is one roving game which is excellent preparation for hunting situations. Judo points were invented for this game because they're almost impossible to lose under grass and

Shooting with friends is the best way to practice.

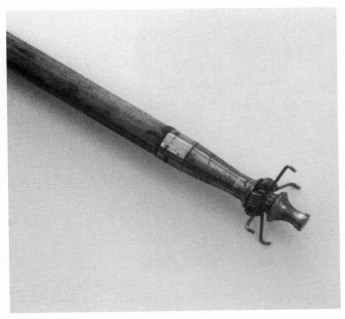

Judo point.

leaves. One shooter chooses a target, such as a leaf or tuft of grass, at any distance and gives the rules for that shot, "you have to have one knee on the ground." He can make the shot as outlandish or as simple as he likes. Everyone shoots one arrow and the one closest to the chosen spot gets a point and selects the next target. We usually play to five points. An hour of shooting in this manner will give you a true measure of how your shooting stacks up under field conditions and highlight where you need further practice.

Steve Dollar, a marvelous shot on game, has come up with a practice tactic for focusing your energies on a deer at the moment of truth. Before you go to work every morning, walk out to your target, concentrate, and fire one arrow. Only one. Leave the arrow in the target, unstring your bow, and go to work. You'll have to live with that one arrow all day, just like you would had it been a shot at a deer. When you get home in the evening go through your normal practice routine. This one-arrow-in-the-morning ploy makes you concentrate on one arrow, shot cold, just like in a real hunting situation. After a couple of weeks it's wonderful how this technique improves

your first arrow accuracy. As the season approaches, this single arrow should be one of your hunting broadheads.

Don't practice three or four times a week all summer and early fall and hone your accuracy to a fine edge, then stop shooting once you enter the woods. You should practice every day while in hunting camp (the only exception being when you're too busy processing a deer). I always carry one judo point in my hunting quiver. Before leaving a stand I'll pick a leaf on the ground and shoot that one arrow. If you've practiced correctly all year up until then, you'll usually hit exactly where you aimed. This goes a long way toward maintaining confidence in your ability, a factor which cannot be overemphasized. If you're *certain* you can make the shot, you'll almost always make it. If you *wonder* if you can make the shot, you most likely won't. To boost confidence and to get the season started right, I'll generally crop the first doe at which I get a chance. A perfect initial shot here lays the foundation toward later perfect shots on bucks.

If you're bothered by buck fever when deer are near (and who isn't), practice drawing on does and small bucks which you don't intend to shoot. This not only helps you learn what you can get away with at close range but the familiarity also helps dampen the adrenaline overload. *Everyone* gets buck fever, it's just that those with more experience are able to hold themselves together until *after* the shot before succumbing to the knee-buckling shakes. Drawing arrows at lots of deer helps a hunter hold off the shakes when he draws an arrow with the deadly intent of releasing it.

Some can make shot after shot on a target at thirty or forty yards, but the margin for error is much greater in the woods. A deer can take a step, or a slight miscalculation by the shooter can send an arrow off target by a couple of feet. Your maximum range is wherever you can place nine out of ten arrows into a one foot circle. Whatever this range turns out to be, please chisel it into granite that you won't take a farther shot at a deer. It's much better to play it close to the vest and try him again on another day than to risk a long shot and either spook him with a miss or, far, far worse, wound a deer with a marginal hit and be unable to find him. Prepare yourself ahead of time to pass on deer that are too far, too alert, too small of antler, or present

Dave Kerkove proved himself a true sportsman when he passed a marginal shot at this Iowa buck. A week later, his discipline was rewarded when the 300# trophy stepped into the open at fifteen yards.

only a bad angle. It takes discipline, true, but the discipline and difficulty are what attracted most hunters to longbows and recurves in the first place.

Be ready as soon as you get into a stand. A few seasons back, as I climbed onto the platform of a treestand, attached the safety harness, and leisurely arranged my gear, a nice buck materialized from thin air. Feeling a little like Howard Hill, I quickly whipped an arrow from my back quiver—and immediately cut the bowstring with the razor-sharp broadhead. Unarmed then and even more harmless than usual, I watched the buck for five straight minutes as he milled about below. Unlike yours truly on that occasion, be prepared when you first enter a stand, for sometimes your movement into an area causes the deer to circle downwind trying to keep track of your location. When you vanish up a tree, they might offer a shot.

Though it's not easy to stay focused for hours while sitting on a stand, it pays to be ready should a deer's appearance surprise you, as it often will. Once a deer is within range is not the time to be fumbling with arrows or shifting position. I always wait with an arrow nocked and the index finger of my left hand holding it in place on the bow. Usually, too, I'll hold the arrow's nock on the string with my right hand, ready to draw on an instant's notice with the least unnecessary movement possible.

Some never shoot at a deer except from a sitting position. I prefer to be standing with one knee braced against the seat when making a shot from a treestand, for it gives me more flexibility to turn and shoot to the right or far around to the left if the deer take unplanned paths. A walking deer generally makes enough noise to help cover the sound of your shot and also seems more relaxed. A nervous deer will stand stock-still, every sense on hyper-alert. It's usually better to wait until he relaxes or begins walking again, for an alert, suspicious deer will jump at the first movement or sound, and his reflexes are quick enough that he's usually gone by the time the arrow arrives.

Once you decide to shoot, don't look at the antlers again. Ignore them. Look only at the spot where the arrow will go. Focus like a laser on one tuft of hair and try to split it with your broadhead. It sounds simple but this is one of the most difficult things to remember as you draw an arrow. If you think to

The chances of killing this deer with an arrow are slim. A bad hit or a miss are far more likely. Better to wait until he relaxes or try him again on another day.

yourself, "But I don't want a spot, I want the whole deer," and simply launch an arrow in his direction you're almost certain to miss, usually by shooting high. I write this from sad, personal experience. This is where all of the focused practice comes in; if you're used to picking a tiny spot on a target you're likely to do the same on a deer, even when you're heart rate approaches three hundred.

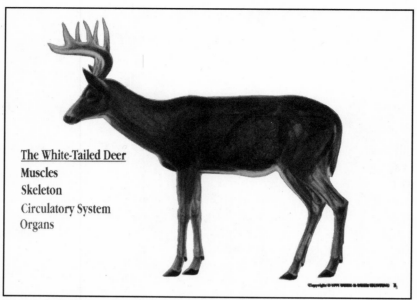

Essential whitetail anatomy chart.

Our grandpas always told us to "shoot 'em right behind the shoulder," and this was good advice with a precision firearm and telescopic sight. But, surprisingly, this isn't where you should aim with a bow. Sure, if your arrow goes exactly where you're looking behind the shoulder you shoot him in the heart, but this shot offers a very thin margin for error. Two or three inches farther back and its into the liver or paunch. *Deer and Deer Hunting Magazine* markets a deer anatomy chart (which every bowhunter should own), with clear plastic overlays showing muscles, skeleton, circulatory system, and organs. Studying this chart is very revealing, for not one bowhunter in ten can correctly place heart, lungs, liver, and spine. The center of the vitals is directly in line with the front leg and about a third of the way up the body. Most hunters think the shoulder bones and shoulder blade cover this area but they don't; the leg and shoulder bones angle forward and the shoulder blade sits much higher, toward the top of the back. If you aim directly up the leg, there is about a one foot diameter area of lungs, heart, and major arteries. An arrow placed anywhere within this area is remarkably lethal, usually killing in a matter of four or five seconds.

FOLLOWING THE SHOT

After shooting at a deer, try to recreate in your mind exactly where the arrow struck. It's difficult sometimes, when your brain's scrambled like an egg and your heart's on fast forward, to remember precisely what happened. But while sitting and waiting for the shakes to subside, slowly replay the sequence of events; the deer's approach, how you drew the bow, where the arrow struck and at what angle, how far it penetrated (there are times when an arrow will back out of a wound as a deer spins to run, making it look as though there was very little penetration), what you heard after the deer disappeared, and the exact spot where you last saw the deer. These matters are all vitally important when deciding how to follow a wounded animal.

Remember the anatomy chart. If you are certain the arrow struck in the one foot diameter kill zone then you can wait fifteen minutes and follow your deer. Once the deer disappeared, if the sound of his running suddenly stopped, or was accompanied by crashing or thrashing before stopping, you can proceed directly to where you heard the last sound and be sure that he'll be right there. An arrow placed in the engine room usually kills within seconds, and a deer rarely travels much over a hundred yards.

If unsure of the arrow's location, which is sometimes the case with dark fletching, or marginal light conditions, or a deer's movement just as the arrow arrives, wait fifteen minutes then very quietly examine the area where the deer was standing. If you find your arrow, or part of it, try to determine how much it penetrated. Sniff the arrow or any blood on the ground. A liver hit has that distinctive liver odor, a hit in the paunch smells like a recently gutted deer, and a hit in the intestines more like fresh manure. If you can find blood, examine it carefully. Thin, watery blood with particles of vegetation often indicates a paunch hit. Blood which contains fecal matter means guts.

Bright red blood or frothy blood points to a lung shot. Great amounts of blood indicate an artery has been cut.

If there are indications of a lung or arterial hit, begin following the trail immediately. If still unsure of the arrow's placement, back out of the area or wait quietly for at least an hour before taking up the trail. If, however, you're now fairly sure of a liver, paunch, or gut shot, you have some decisions to make. A deer hit in such a manner usually lies down within two hundred yards and often within fifty. He'll probably expire right there *if he's not jumped.* If you follow too soon and scare him up, he might well run another half mile, likely without leaving much, if any, blood trail which means the chances of recovery have now plummeted to near zero. Ideally, a deer with a marginal though fatal wound should be left alone for at least five or six hours, although weather and ground conditions play a factor in the decision. With snow on the ground, such a deer is much easier to follow and you may want to begin sooner. If the weather is very warm, as it often is during bow season in the south, the meat of a dead deer can spoil in a matter of hours, so you may not want to wait. If rain or snow is eminent, the trail should be followed without delay. But if the weather is cold, with no precipitation, waiting until daylight to follow such a deer shot at dusk is the best plan.

A lung or heart shot might leave an almost solid stream of blood, a trail the rankest beginner could follow with one eye closed. But even a perfectly placed shot sometimes leaves surprisingly little blood to follow, especially if the shot was at a downward angle and there was no exit wound. At these times, as with marginal hits, every ounce of our woodsmanship, perseverance, intuition, and, yes, love for the deer must be brought into play as we follow the trail.

Two people are ideal for following a wounded deer. One stays on the actual trail of blood splatters or tracks. The other walks just behind and to one side and watches both ahead ten or fifteen feet for obvious sign and constantly scans the woods for the wounded or dead deer. The trackers should move quietly, talking only in whispers to prevent spooking the deer if he's still alive. For night-time tracking, nothing beats one of the rechargeable spotlights, three hundred to five hundred

A rechargeable 300,000 candlepower portable spotlight. Every bowhunting camp needs a couple of these.

thousand candlepower. These powerful lights will last an hour or longer with the optional extended battery packs, usually more than enough time to find a mortally hit deer. Each tracker should have his own spotlight.

On a tough trail when the apparent sign runs out, you'll be searching not for drops of blood but for specks the size of the period at the end of this sentence. Or faint smears rubbed on tall grass stems. You are not only tracking blood or footprints, but disturbance in leaves or grass, as well. Both trackers should be on hands and knees at these times, being careful not to get ahead of the last certain sign and possibly obscure some unseen trace. It's important to try to stay with the physical thread of the deer's passing, as it's often very difficult to pick up the thread once it's lost or abandoned. I once followed and recovered a deer shot through one lung who turned at right angles to cross a fence, traveled a hundred yards, then turned again at right angles to recross the same fence before crashing in thick brush fifty yards beyond. Such an evasive maneuver is almost impossible to follow if you lose the physical trail. When a trail becomes difficult, small pieces of toilet paper should be used to mark tracks or blood. The visual line of the paper can help you predict where the next sign should be.

If, however, the sign should finally dwindle to nothing after meticulous examination, as it sometimes will, stick an arrow beside the last drop of blood or track. The trackers move forward slowly, one a few feet on each side of the line of the trail. Scrutinize every leaf and every blade of grass for the smallest speck of blood and search for disturbances in leaves or dirt, for a running deer will leave some evidence on all but the hardest ground. Be especially alert for the possibility of the deer turning sharply, for when a trail is lost it's often because the deer turned. If nothing is found after twenty or thirty yards of searching, return to the arrow marking the last physical sign, switch sides, and cover the same ground again, only more slowly this time.

If the trail is lost even after such a hands-and-knees search, start again at the arrow. With the direction of the last known trail at twelve o'clock, one tracker should go twenty or thirty yards toward seven o'clock and the other twenty or thirty yards toward five o'clock. Circle forward, staying about thirty yards from the arrow, toward the last line of the trail, assuming that the deer has turned and one of them will cross his path. If nothing is found, the maneuver is repeated at about fifty yards. Then seventy-five. Then a hundred. Most often the trail will be intersected and the follow-up continued.

If the trail still cannot be found, return to the arrow and appraise what the deer could see from that spot. Is there thick brush in one direction? A wounded deer often heads for the thickest jungle he can find. We've all read that wounded deer travel downhill, and sometimes they do, but in my experience they're far more interested in cover and will travel up a slope to reach it. If the trail is lost in fairly open country and heavy cover is within sight, it's a good bet that's where the deer headed. If you're familiar with a place, use your knowledge of any nearby thick cover within two or three hundred yards, and check it carefully. Any nearby fence should also be searched for sign of the deer's crossing. Deer well know that men can be left behind by crossing a fence and use this fact to their advantage. A ranch road, creek, powerline, or other linear obstruction which crosses the deer's last know line of travel should be slowly walked. This past season, I reacquired a deer's trail by finding a tiny splotch of blood on grass stems where he crossed a jeep road through the woods.

If you know you placed a fatal arrow into a deer, redouble your efforts if conventional tracking methods have failed. As Winston Churchhill once said in another context, "Never give up. Never. Never. Never." Walk a zigzag pattern along and either side of the last line of travel. More help than the original two trackers is valuable now because additional people can thoroughly cover more ground looking primarily for the downed deer but also for blood or tracks. Use your nose, too, for on a couple of occasions when passing downwind I have smelled the odor of a dead deer before finding him.

In most cases on a marginal hit or on a wounded deer which was earlier jumped and never recovered, the hunters failed to go far enough. Your maps can often be useful when planning the area and distance to search. Consider where the wounded deer likely came from and his normal travel avenues. He will often retrace his steps because he knows the route is safe. If you're sure you have a fatal hit, persistence is the key. Few things are more nerve-racking or intense than following a wounded deer, but few things are more important. Nothing is more satisfying than finding one after a difficult search, and nothing gives the anti-hunters more ammo than giving up on one which was mortally hit.

Despite our best efforts, on rare occasion we are still unable to find a wounded deer. Sometimes the wound is fatal and we simply never find the animal and sometimes the deer recovers from the arrow. There is no disgrace if an exhaustive search was made but we should all learn from our mistakes. Redouble your practice to become a better shot. Vow to show more discipline and shoot only in perfect situations. Keep your broadheads shaving sharp in the field and use them with heavy arrows. Study and practice to become a better tracker.

In the same vein, always check every missed shot. It's not officially a miss until you've found your arrow and it has no trace of blood or hair. At times, we've found blood and later the deer when a hunter was certain it was a miss. Conversely, we've also found pristine arrows buried under grass, proving a clean miss, when the hunter swore the wounded deer ran off with it. Too much adrenaline can be almost psychedelic, especially in those with little experience, though veterans can be afflicted, too, myself included. Always check misses, without exception.

PROFESSOR WHITETAIL

⸘

The sun melted into the horizon, making the trees and grass and deer glow with a perfect, radiant light. The doe and two yearlings had suddenly appeared out of the creekbed and now filtered among the trees like gray wisps of smoke. After ten minutes of casual browsing, they finally worked their way past me through the shooting lane and on toward the wheat field another quarter mile away. I let them pass my tree unaware, holding out for the mature buck I knew was also using the funnel. Even this early in the season, mid-October before the rut, he was most likely veteran enough not to show himself in the daytime. Patiently, though, I waited for him, knowing that if enough time was piled up the scales of success might be tipped in my favor. Tonight's wait was part of the investment required for a close encounter with such a deer.

I wondered if Lee, my eldest son of fifteen, was having similar thoughts. Probably not, for he had endured several seasons of missed shots and wanted badly to draw blood, never having taken a deer with a bow. Nor had Reed, my thirteen-year-old son, though he, too, had missed or alerted deer with his motion and noise several times each of the past three seasons. Early on, I worried about their competitive natures, each striving to beat his brother by taking that first deer. The competition had quickly faded, however, for even with their limited experience they had come to understand that the contest was not between individuals, but between the hunter and the deer. If they became hooked on bowhunting and stayed with it into adulthood, they would eventually come to understand that the competition—the strategy and practice and learning to control their excitement when the time came for a shot—was mostly within themselves. . .

I had yet to actually see the buck I was hunting. His rubs on thigh-thick trees had initially betrayed his presence and closer inspection of the area had revealed couple of faint trails and an occasional track leading to a twenty acre cedar thicket on a hillside. With the rut yet to come and knowing where the buck lived, I had a few tricks in store for him before the end of the season.

With the light quickly fading and the first stars appearing, I replaced the razor-sharp hunting arrow in the quiver and withdrew a judo point. I chose a leaf on the ground below and drew, anchored, and released in one slow, fluid motion. Hearing a soft "pop" as the leaf was pinned to the earth, I gathered my gear, unhooked the safety harness, and climbed down. After retrieving the judo point, I started the hike in the darkness to a gate where I had earlier separated from Lee.

Lee's stand overlooked an area of heavy deer activity, a staging area adjacent to the wheat field, while Reed had chosen a distant oak flat where the deer were hustling the limited acorn crop. Conditions had been ideal this evening, with a steady, moderate breeze, so I hoped one of the boys had finally connected after all their frustrated efforts. There was only one way to learn, and Professor Whitetail would illustrate his teachings when the boys moved too soon, or made a noise, or most of all let the adrenaline deluge distort their shooting—as their father still did occasionally.

I'm not sure what it is about big whitetail bucks that is so awe inspiring, what it is that makes otherwise sober, rational people mutter incoherently after a close hunting encounter. But for sure mature bucks can have a unique, paralyzing effect. . .

A friend of mine, Lionel Atwill, had a recent lesson from the good Professor. Understand that Lionel has had decades of experience hunting all over the world, everything from wart hogs to caribou. He served in Special Forces in Vietnam and has some stories which would make Alfred Hitchcock an insomniac. Lionel is not a man prone to hyperventilation. He executed a flawless stalk on a trophy buck, quite a feat in itself, but ruefully admits that that was the last thing he did right. The deer finally stood, broadside, at eighteen yards. Normally a deadly, deliberate shot with a bow, Lionel instantly reared back and launched an arrow in the general direction of the deer. At no time in its flight did said arrow come within five feet of the buck, who simply stared in astonishment at the thoroughly disconcerted hunter before trotting away.

Many hunters are just as stricken when they do get a deer. I have to confess that I'm one of them. Once, I watched a nice buck approach from a distance for thirty minutes, and through Herculean effort somehow maintained my composure as he slowly made his way closer. I finally executed a textbook shot when he ventured within range. Only then did I fall completely apart, trying to draw breath with gaping mouth like a beached carp. I had to wait another hour for a friend to make a pre-arranged pickup, an entire hour for my heart rate to slow and my hands to quit shaking. I was totally back to normal, or so I thought, having stopped drooling and everything. As the jeep at last approached, I feigned nonchalance, the cool, deadly hunter. This would be great.

My friend pulled alongside, took one look at me and blurted, "What's wrong?"

"Nothing," I said, wondering how my serene cover had been blown, "I got a buck."

"Oh," said he, blowing out a long whistle in relief, "from the way you looked I thought you'd been bit by a snake."

Lucky he hadn't seen me an hour earlier, before I'd calmed down.

Professor Whitetail may have an even more electrifying effect on the less experienced. Sherry Crow, the wife of a regular hunting companion, Ted Crow, last season had her first encounter with a mature, bull-of-the-woods whitetail buck one morning. The result was a missed easy shot. A short time later, when Ted arrived to pick her up, Sherry was draped around a fencepost, ashen.

"What's the matter?" Ted asked, genuinely concerned.

"I don't know, but I feel awful." Sherry shook her head. "I think I've had a stroke."

Ted quickly felt her forehead, checking for temperature.

"It started when I shot at that deer," she stammered.

"What deer?"

"The biggest buck I've ever seen," she managed, "just thinking about it makes me dizzy."

Ted took a step back, eyeing her carefully.

Noticing his spreading grin, she insisted, "This is serious. I need to see a doctor."

"A doctor can't cure buck fever."

"Buck fever? You're crazy. This must've been some sort of heart attack."

Ted's smile threatened to erupt into full-blown laughter.

"It's not a bit funny," she said, the color slowly returning to her cheeks.

Ted finally doubled up about then, hands on knees, making only a strangled "whew-whew" sound occasionally. From what I understand, it took him awhile, between laughing fits, to convince his wife that she did, indeed, have buck fever rather than some life-threatening condition. The buck fever must have somehow affected her vocal chords, though, because she didn't speak to him the rest of that day. . .

I reached the gate a couple of minutes before Lee, and could sense the pent-up tension in his steps as he approached.

"Well?" I prompted.

"I hit one," he said simply, unstringing his longbow.

"Tell it from the start."

He explained in a shaky voice that a doe and a yearling had approached his stand just before dark. The doe passed at the limits of his range, so he waited, motionless, until the yearling was in his shooting lane at fifteen yards. He picked a spot and released, and thought the arrow was into the kill zone, angling down and forward. The deer bolted into the brush but the sound of its running ended abruptly after a few seconds. Unsure exactly what had transpired, Lee waited until dark then climbed down quietly and headed for our meeting place.

"You did good," I assured him.

We returned to his treestand and found a couple of drops of blood where the deer had been standing. The blood trail increased as we followed, until our small flashlights finally picked out the deer, dead less than a hundred yards from Lee's tree.

"Alright," he said, as we darted to the deer.

I grabbed his hand and shook it.

"Alright," he said again, a grin threatening to split his face.

He had called his shot correctly on the yearling doe, right in the engine room, a clean, quick kill. Kneeling, he placed a hand on the deer, then glanced up.

"You know, most people don't realize how hard this is."

I was aware that because he chose to hunt, he had withstood a certain amount of pressure from his high school peers. A few of them loudly upheld the notion that no one should hunt anything at any time, that all wildlife hung by a thread over the abyss of extinction. Such zealots, whether young or old, generally covered their ears when anyone tried to introduce a few facts to the discussion, such as there were just as many deer now as when Columbus landed, or that hunters' efforts were largely responsible for their present numbers. . .

Lee seemed delighted but mildly stunned, scarcely believing that he had finally become predator enough to take a deer on its own terms. I had introduced him to Professor Whitetail as my father had me so many years before. I knew Lee's lifelong outdoor education was in good hands.

APPENDIX

Bear River Treestands
3110 Ranchview Ln.
Minneapolis, MN 55447
800/536-3337

Big Buck Treestands
855 Chicago Rd.
Quincy, MI 49082
517/639-3815

Butler's
(complete line of traditional archery
supplies)
163 Bear River Dr.
Evanston, WY 82930
307/789-4982

Deer and Deer Hunting Magazine
(whitetail anatomy chart)
700 E. State St.
Iola, WI 54990
715/445-2214

Kustom King
(complete line of traditional archery
supplies)
1260 E. 86th Pl.
Merrillville, IN 46410
219/769-6640

L.L. Bean
(camo and fleece clothing, outdoor
equipment)
Freeport, ME 04033
800/221-4221

Legend Videos
(aging and judging deer video)
1000 Campbell Rd #208-111
Houston, TX 77055
800/346-0465

Northwest Archery
(St. Charles quivers)
19807 1st Ave. South
Seattle, WA 91848
206/878-7300

Predator Camo
2605 Coulee Ave.
La Crosse, WI 54601
608/787-0551

Rancho Safari
(Catquivers and Shaggie Suit)
PO Box 691
Ramona, CA 92065
619/789-2094

Screaming Eagle
(Swandri and Filson wool clothing)
100 Greensburgh Rd.
New Kensington, PA 15068
412/339-2352

Skyline Camo
184 Ellicott Rd.
West Falls, NY 14170
800/997-7955

Swarovski Optik
One Wholesale Way
Cranston, RI 02920
800/426-3089

Three Rivers Archery
(complete line of traditional archery
supplies)
PO Box 517
Ashley, IN 46705
219/587-9501

Trophy Whitetail Treestands
329 E. Shockley Ferry Rd.
Anderson, SC 29624
864/231-9506

Tru-Angle Sharpening Hones
6658 S. St. Road 13
Wabash, IN 46992
800/854-8942

Wedge-Loc Treestands
1760 Hubert Rd.
Midland, MI 48640
517/835-3856

Zeiss Optical
1015 Commerce St.
Petersburg, VA 23803
804/861-0033

Every fall, the author conducts bowhunting clinics
in some of the prime whitetail areas of
North America. Contact us for dates.

PO Box 233
Azle, TX 76098
817/237-0829

Send a long SASE for a free catalog of our
traditional archery titles.